A Soldier's Journey with The Presence of God

ARTHUR DAVID JR.

ISBN 978-1-63844-705-4 (paperback)
ISBN 978-1-63844-706-1 (digital)

Christian Faith Publishing, Inc.
832 Park Avenue
Meadville, PA 16335
www.christianfaithpublishing.com

Printed in the United States of America

My name is Arthur David Jr. or Poncho as all my family and childhood friends would call me. When I was born, some said that I looked Mexican. My Uncle Joe thought I looked like the Mexican on the cowboy show called *The Cisco Kid*. His sidekick was called Poncho and thought it would be cute to call me Poncho. Little did he know at the time that it would stick and become my nickname. You can imagine how this might cause me to become a little headstrong and really outgoing. As I grew, I often found myself in situations that provided me the opportunity to try to control outcomes. This need to control would lead me down a road of self-discovery that eventually helped me realize what my life's purpose was. Some people might call my stories a series of miracles. But I look at it as God's way of saying it's not your time.

I heard him saying, "I have a special purpose for you. Now, I want you to allow me to take you on a journey into life-threatening situations that will build your confidence in me and along the way reveal my purpose for you."

I feel compelled to share these stories in hopes that you might discover the same presence of God and his continual loving presence in your life.

I'm dedicating this book to my wife, Cathy, and my mother, Jeri. It is because of their love and belief in me that I am the man I am today and that I came to find my true self, which is the total sum of who we are and what we are truly here for. Cathy and I have been married for forty-five years, and it is because of her unfailing love, support, and confidence in me that I continued to pursue my true purpose in life and eventually lead me to write this book. I pray that it gives you the same encouragement to pursue *your* true purpose in life. I am convinced that my mission is to help others get closer to God, and with his help, they might begin to find their own true purpose in life. God wants us all to feel his unconditional love and forgiveness as we allow him to work in and through us, and along the way, we might just discover who we were created to be.

I want to thank my brother, Rick, for helping me cowrite this book. It's because of his God-given talents that helped bring my feelings and past experiences to life in each and every chapter. Also, a big thanks to my son, Jeff, and my daughter, Kim, for all their time and talents in making this book the best it can be.

A heartfelt thanks to my literary agent, Linda, project manager, Scott, including the whole staff at the Christian Faith Publishing Company.

PREFACE

My purpose for writing this book is to touch the hearts of those who are in doubt about a higher power or, should I say, the presence of God. I found God through a series of life-threatening events that he delivered me from when I was a soldier fighting in Vietnam in 1967–68. Through these stories in this book, may you be lead to think about your relationship with God. I was snatched from the jaws of death three times, by the grace of God, so that I was able to return home and face the challenges of a changed world. With all the sickness, disasters, and evil that was in the world then and still exists today, it's only natural that we question the love of God. We all have doubts about God and Jesus Christ.

I know I sure did, even though I was raised Catholic.

My whole life growing up, I went to Catholic schools, and I went to church every Sunday, as well as all the holy days and holidays. As a young child, I was just going through the motions doing what I was told to do. This was the norm for most of us that grew up at that time. Making all the sacraments and learning all the prayers still didn't help me get any closer to God, let alone truly believe in him.

I was born on December 4, 1946. We were the first wave of the baby boomers. I had the hardest time growing up and believing that there was a God that truly cared about *me*, especially when I turned nineteen and got drafted into the Army. I was sent to Vietnam knowing that as a soldier in a combat zone, there would be death all around me every day. Little did I know that later I would be coming home to a country filled with people that hated me for fighting for a cause I believed in with all my heart, something called "our freedom." Knowing what was going on at that time with all the protests, rioting, shooting, and looting would cause you to wonder, what is our world coming to. Everyone was going crazy with all kinds of mixed feelings. Some people thought we shouldn't be in the war, others refusing to be drafted and fleeting to Canada. With college students all over the country protesting the war, anger and hatred started to build.

After being home for only a few months, I began feeling a sense of rejection from my wife. Only being nineteen and twenty, we were still young adults trying to find our purpose in life. We thought we were doing everything a newlywed couple should do in order to be happy. But being apart for two years didn't help. And living in such different environments, we began taking two different paths. Being married for only four weeks before shipping out didn't help either. We never really had the chance to get to know each other. Only a few months after I was discharged, we found ourselves pulling apart. We both believed that because we were married in the Catholic Church, we shouldn't get divorced. So as an alternative, we decided to go to Catholic Social Services for marriage counseling. That didn't help at all. We thought that maybe if we had a child, things would change. We would have a common goal. However, after our daughter Kimberly, was born, it became quite clear that even the deep love we both had for her couldn't salvage our broken relationship. Two short years later, my wife told me she no longer loved me and wanted to be on her own. We got a divorce. These were very trying times for me. Knowing I wouldn't get to see my beautiful little daughter Kimmy every morning devastated me. I was wondering why God spared me from a brutal war only to deliver me into a world that seemed to not want to have anything to do with me. This pushed me into a deeper depression, leaving me angry, bitter, and confused. All I could think of was how I lost everything: my wife, my child, my job, my friends, my family, and belief in myself.

Why was this happening? Did something happen to me? Did this series of life-altering experiences cause me to become some kind of monster that no one could love? Or was it that the world had changed so drastically in the past two years that I no longer fit? What do I do now? I became a very bitter person who was deeply depressed, self-centered, hurt, and angry for a very long time. This caused me to not trust anyone for fear of rejection. Unfortunately, the mistakes I made along the way hurt a lot of people and I became a very selfish person. Somehow, along the way, God took me to a place where I had to learn to forgive myself. I asked God to help me find the right words in order to share the painful lessons I have learned so that others might be able to relate. My desire is to touch the hearts of all those who find themselves in similar circumstances, and maybe feeling the same way I did—lost, alone, angry at God, and not having a real purpose in life.

By showing you what I went through and how I weathered every storm in my life, I hope and pray that you will also find the joy and peace that can only be found in Jesus Christ. Not only IS there a God, but he CARES. He is alive, and he is with us every moment. Watching out for us and waiting for a chance to be a part of our everyday lives. He is here to protect us and to give us a life with purpose.

He has shown me several times in my life that he is here and truly cares by granting me the miracles that saved my life. And now, I am privileged to be able to share them with you in the following chapters. You will see how life can change in a split second. When you can't see any way out and turn to him, he's there to show you the way. All you need to do is ask him in prayer with your whole heart, mind, and soul, then he will answer. He always answers, because he has a purpose for every one of us and he has a purpose for you too! Just ask him!

Bible verse to think about—Matthew 7:7–8: "Ask, and it shall be given to you; seek, and you shall find; knock, and it shall be open to you. For everyone who asks, receives; and who seeks, finds; and to him who knocks, it shall be opened."

INTRODUCTION

Growing up in the sixties was a very fast-paced life for all of us with fast cars, rock and roll, garage bands, the Vietnam War, protests, and hippies. After high school, I was drafted in the army and sent to fight in the Vietnam War. Over the next four years, I fought a war, was married, and had a child. From 1965 to 1969, life was filled with turmoil. I was looking forward to a future filled with all the good things life had to offer. Then it all started to unravel. Just when I thought life was going to be great, God brought me home from a war where I lost many of my army buddies, family, home, and career. Yet God for some reason spared me from death or injury. On the first day back home, my wife told me my mom and dad got divorced. Two years later, my wife told me she wanted a divorce! I sank into a deep depression, feeling like everyone gave up on me. I was losing my wife, child, career, and house, and learned my parents were divorced. I saw buddies killed in the war and came home to a country that hated me. They greeted me at the airport by spitting at me and calling me "Baby Killer!" It seemed almost more than I could take.

They didn't have a name for it at the time, but what I discovered later is that I had PTSD (post-traumatic stress disorder). With no help in sight, it took me a very long time to get through it. But with the grace of God, a lot of therapy, and staying close to family and friends, I found peace in my heart. Even today, when I feel a little anxiety coming on,

I find I need to do some deep breathing therapy, and then I immediately start to feel calmer and more relaxed. This works for me, but might not work for you. So find whatever works for you by seeking help.

In the following chapters, you will read about how I dealt with the feelings of anger, depression, and guilt. At the end of each story, you will see a section on "Life Lesson Learned." This is where I discovered why God put challenges in front of me. Then I shared a "Bible verse" for you to meditate on and find a sense of peace, understanding, and direction. I believe that God reveals himself through his Word, through others, and through our life experiences. I've combined all three in each chapter to help you understand how he communicated to me.

CHAPTER 1

Signs from God

My story starts in 1964 when I was a junior at Shrine of the Little Flower High School in Royal Oak, Michigan. During the summer, I would be working with my dad and my uncle at Ray White Electric Company. They had me working in several areas of the company. First, I started in the stockroom and then I moved to shipping and receiving. After some time, they trained me in the wire-cutting department, setting up the cutting and the terminal machines. I could see why my dad had me working in so many areas of the business. It was because my dad, Art David Sr., and my uncle, Ed David, had made plans to start a business on their own. They wanted me to be part of it, which made me feel excited just thinking that I would be a major player in our family's business.

After graduating in 1965, I accepted their offer and began working in a six-thousand-square-foot building that my uncle rented in Roseville, Michigan. I started the task of building an electrical component and wire harness business that was known as DC Electronics. They were still working for Ray White Electric at the time and weren't ready yet to quit. My dad was a supervisor for the wire cutting and electrical component department, and my uncle was an outside salesman who was in personal contact with all the customers and their buyers. They planned on joining me and take over their new business once I got the company up and running. I dove in and dedicated all my time and energy completely alone until they could leave their current positions and join me.

My first day, I got in a truckload of wire of all sizes and different gauges delivered. Next, I had to lay out a stockroom and put everything in order according to size, color, gauges, and types of wire. The following day, I received a truck full of wire terminals and wire grommets. Again, back to setting up the stock in the stockroom in a numeric order by size and wire gauge. For the next two weeks, I would get in some lumber to build five layout tables. It was my job to set up work for the employees on the wire cutting and terminal machines, plus set up all the work stations, stockroom, receive and organize all the inventory so that in the summer of June 1966, the business would be ready for my dad and uncle to take it over full-time. Finally, after numerous hours of hard work and bordering on exhaustion, I found myself being lead to my first of many encounters with God's amazing grace.

Needless to say, after working eight to ten hours a day, five days a week, and then partying every night with my two high school buddies (Dominic and Mike), I was extremely exhausted by the end of the week. I just turned nineteen, and my girlfriend Nancy Bennett moved to Akron, Ohio, with her whole family. By this time, we had been dating for two years and were certain this was true love. She was all I could think about. How was I supposed to go for an entire two weeks without being with her? Unthinkable! So we made arrangements for me to drive down to see her every other weekend. Her mom and dad both said it would be okay if I stayed at their house when I came to visit.

After driving back and forth for about six months, the drive became very routine. I felt I could drive it in my sleep.

Little did I know I was about to get my chance to prove it. One freezing weekend in January, I was excited to see Nancy again, so I left work early and headed home to pack. I got a bite to eat, took a hot shower, grabbed my overnight bag, and headed for the living room to say goodbye to my mom. She was watching the news and told me she just heard the weather report on TV and that a snow storm was expected to hit Ohio and would dump four to six inches of snow across the entire state. This included Akron, but it should be over by 6:00 p.m. She questioned whether I should make the drive tonight. I assured her with only a three hour drive not to worry. By the time I get there, it should be all over and the roads should be plowed. Besides, it was mostly all expressways to her house anyway. It was about two weeks since the last time we saw each other, and I really wanted to see her. I found that it is true: "absence does make the heart grow fonder."

I was on the road by 6:30 p.m. and after driving for more than two hours in the dark with snow flurries floating down so very slowly, I began to become mesmerized. It was almost like they were dancing on my windshield to the slow song I had playing on the radio. The steady rhythmic slap of the wipers only helped relax away any tension I may have been feeling. *Maybe I should have listened to Mom*, I thought. However, the roads were salted and just wet, so I assured myself that I was totally in control. I was getting very sleepy, however. That hot shower really did relax me, and the music on the radio was soft and soothing. The warm air from the heater was only contributing to this formula for disaster. I found it extremely hard to keep my eyes open. I was thinking about what we were going to do that weekend and where we were going to go. I was driving on I-80 doing about sixty-five miles an hour. I was about an hour outside of Akron, when something extremely strange happened. I must have fallen asleep.

But when I opened my eyes, I remember seeing the clock on the dashboard that read 10:35 p.m. I asked myself, *How can that be? I should have been to Nancy's by 9:30 p.m. What happened to the last two hours of my life? And where am I?* I strangely found myself in a world that made no sense at all. When I looked around, nothing made sense. There was no traffic. No headlights. No road. I was no longer driving. Everything was peaceful and quiet. All the windows were blanketed in white. The front window, the side windows, and the back window were completely covered. At that point I was totally confused I thought to myself, *I must be dead!* Not understanding and completely disoriented, I thought to myself, *I'm in my car and its running. The heater's on and the radio is on. What is going on? I was just driving my car on I-80 going to Akron.* Now I wake up to, "God only knows!" I didn't know if I fell asleep or for how long. I couldn't have crashed, because I was feeling just fine. So what is going on? I was confused! So I decided to roll down my window to see what was all over the windows. I reached out to feel what this was—fog, smoke, or just a haze. To my surprise it was *snow*. I must be buried in snow somewhere. But where and how did I get there without feeling the car crash? Not even waking me up from a sleep! And how long was I asleep before I woke up?

Next, I shut the car off realizing that I could kill myself from carbon monoxide poisoning if it started to back up in the car. Then I turned back to my window and rolled it all the way down and started to dig my way out. After only digging a short time, I realized that the car was only partially buried, nose down in a drainage ditch on the side of the expressway. When I reached the top of my car, I crawled on the roof and walked down to the trunk of the car and jumped off to the roadside. I looked back at my car and realized that I had gone off the road in between two large signs. Call it luck if you want, but I call it the grace of God and my guardian angel who kept me safe without a scratch.

Standing on the side of the expressway, I tried to flag down a car for help, but no one would stop. It must have been about half an hour before a state trooper drove up with his overhead and spotlights on. He got out of his car and said someone saw me stranded on the side of the road and called the station. Because it was so cold, we immediately got in his car. I was told to get in the backseat, while he sat in the front where it was nice and warm. He then pulled out a notebook and asked me for my driver's license and registration. Then he asked me to tell him what happened so he could fill out his report. Before I got started, he asked me where I was going and who he could contact. I gave him my girlfriend's name and her phone number. He called the station and had them call Nancy's dad so he could come to pick me up. After hanging up with the station, he looked in his rearview mirror and said, "Hey, buddy, you must have done something right."

I asked, "What are you talking about?"

"Well," he said, "the way your car just fit between those two big signs, you couldn't have driven it in there if you tried. There must be someone upstairs looking out for you."

At that, I looked out the window and saw my car wedged perfectly between two freeway signs. Chills ran down my spine as the realization came to me that God's hand *had* to be on me. Even Lady Luck could never have delivered me from the fate that was averted only by the grace of God.

Life Lesson Learned

I now know, like it or not, we all have someone watching over us and keeping us out of harm's way. Everything happens for a reason! God moves us in his time, not ours. So when things happen to us that we can't explain, just trust in him, and he will show us in due time that he has a plan for us all.

> "For he will command his angles concerning you to guard you in all your ways" (Psalm 91:11).

CHAPTER 2

Three Encounters in Vietnam

Six months later, I got my draft notice! **UNCLE SAM WANTS YOU!**

I was to report to Fort Wayne, Indiana, on the fourteenth of June 1966, to the induction center where we would get sworn into the Army. The night before leaving for the train station in Detroit to go to Fort Wayne, I went out with my best friend Dominic. We spent all night together drinking a few beers and talking all about my chances of going to Vietnam. We were both really scared that I would end up in the war fighting for not only my country but for my life as well. I can still remember like it was yesterday, sitting in my car with Dom, talking all night long in front of his house. We were talking, laughing, and crying about all the great times we had together and all the time in the back of our minds we would be wondering if I would make it back. We were talking for so long that one of Dom's neighbors called the police saying that there is a strange car parked in front of her household with two guys just sitting there for hours. It must have been three in the morning when a policeman pulled up behind us. He walked up to the car and flashed his light in the car and asked me to roll down my window. He wanted to know what we were doing there and why we were there for so long based on what the neighbor told them. I explained that I got drafted in the Army and was leaving in the morning, and I was just saying goodbye to my buddy. He immediately said, "I understand, and thank you for serving our country. Just take your time but don't be too much longer." At that point, Dom and I decided to call it a night, knowing we were going to only get a couple of hours sleep. The next morning around 7:00 a.m. my whole family and Dom went to the train station to say goodbye. We all hugged, cried, and said our final goodbyes.

A few hours later I boarded the train and settled in for a three-hour ride to Fort Wayne, Indiana. Upon arrival, an army bus transported me to the military base to be processed. After being sworn in, we were shipped down to Fort Knox, Kentucky, where I had my basic training and did my AIT (Advance Individual Training) which was radio school.

The Vietnam War (1959–1975) was bloody, dirty, and very unpopular with everyone. In Vietnam, the US soldiers found themselves fighting an enemy they rarely saw and barley understood. In the jungle, the Vietcong always had the upper hand because this was their home and their life. Most of us, on the other hand, never even saw a jungle except in the movies. This was a completely different world for us. The extreme temperatures and unbearable humidity would melt even the toughest of soldiers. The goal for us guys in the war was to do whatever it took to get our job done, stay safe and get home all in one piece.

This part of the story is about my life as a young man who just graduated from high school and found himself in a war zone twenty-four months later and how I coped with the physical, mental, and spiritual battles as well. It didn't take long for me to comprehend what hell must be like. How people could live every day like this was beyond my imagination. I started every day with a simple prayer: "Dear God, keep me safe. Get me home!"

This story is not so much about the war but how in the midst of all this insanity, God reached down from heaven and through a series of events, took all this evil and used it to reveal his unchanging love for me. The whole time I was searching for the enemy, he revealed to me that my greatest enemy was inside myself. Simply put, I guess you could say in the worst of times, I found the God I had been searching for all my life. Not realizing that he was with me all along. As you follow my journey, keep in mind that this is the same God that cares about you just as much. He is as close as your next breath. All you need to do is to just talk to him. Some call it prayer. Whatever you call it, doesn't matter. Just talk to him. Then, and only then can he help you. It's called free will. He respects our ability to choose freely. Once you do, your life will change in more ways than you could ever imagine. The problem we all have is we take him for granted. We only call on him when we are in trouble. Can you imagine how you would feel if your child never talked to you but only when they had to or when they needed something? You would feel used, hurt, taken for granted, neglected, and maybe feel even unloved. I found myself doing just that. I would only do what I had to do to be a good Christian boy. I would pray before bed, pray before eating, and go to church every Sunday as I was taught my whole life in a strict Catholic environment. Now that I look back, I give thanks to my mother because she ensured that my brother Rick and I had a good Catholic education.

I attended a Catholic grade school at Our Lady of La Salette in Berkley, Michigan, and Shrine High School in

Royal Oak Michigan. With my mother's strong belief in God and my Catholic upbringing, I found myself calling on God as I needed him. Most of us young people that grew up in the sixties found it hard to believe that God was listening to us. After all, there is far too many people who were in worse shape than ourselves. An even if he could hear me, how was he going to talk to me to give me the help or advice I needed? I had so many uncertain feelings about *"God."* So for the rest of my younger years, I would do the least possible as a Catholic just to make sure I was covered, just in case there is a God and a heaven and hell. I guess I looked at it as "fire" insurance. That was because I didn't trust that there was a God. Yet I didn't want to take any chances. After all, I was taught about God by my parents, priests, nuns, and by what I heard in church and school. So, I continued to go through the motions of being a faithful Catholic, just in case. Then it all started happening. I was about to have my first encounter with this God of my childhood who was about to grab me by the collar and shake me to the very core.

Shortly after graduation, I found out that I would be getting drafted in the Army that coming June. My mother asked me to sit down so she could talk to me before leaving for the service. She was quite concerned about me and my safety because of all the young men that were losing their lives in the Vietnam War. She told me that she would be praying for me every day until I returned home. She said that she was saving something for me that would help keep me safe. She reached in her purse and pulled out an old looking holy card. It had a picture of the resurrection of Jesus and three soldiers at his feet covering their eyes from his radiant glow. At the bottom of the card, it read "Easter Greetings;" and on the back in my mother's own handwriting it read, "To Baby Arthur from Mother." I realized in that moment that she kept that card from the moment I was born. It must have been a mother's intuition that made her keep that card until this very moment. When she gave this to me, she said, "Always keep this on you. It will keep you safe because Jesus is our savior and protector."

Holy Card from Art's mother

After finishing my basic training, I returned home, and I asked Nancy to marry me. I thought that if we were engaged to be married while I was away, I wouldn't lose her to someone else. So this way I felt that she would be faithful to me, and I wouldn't have to worry about her. You can tell I was really young and insecure with my own feelings.

Fast forward to the following spring. Nancy and I decided that we would get married in May 1967. We both were confident that I wouldn't be going to Vietnam because after all my training, I was stationed at Fort Lewis Army Base in Washington for six months. For added reassurance, I asked my CO what my chances were on me going to Vietnam; and he said, "Go get married. I don't see it happening for you right now, and the odds are fairly slim." Knowing that, we got married, moved out to Washington, and found a cute little apartment on Fort Lewis Army Base in Pierce, Washington. It wasn't two weeks later that orders came down for me to be shipped out to Vietnam in forty-eight hours.

My whole life changed on June 15, 1967, when I found myself in a place I thought I would never be. In a foreign country fighting a war and encountering death every day and on three separate occasions, narrowly escaping death myself. Not a day would go by that I didn't ask myself, *Why am I here? What is God's plan? Will I get home, or will I die here?* At twenty years old, I found it very scary and very confusing. Thinking to myself, *Can it get any worse?* And to no surprise, it did!

My First Encounter

I was a twenty-year old Army "radio operator" specialist fourth class stationed in Phuc Vinh, Vietnam, in June 1967, the height of the war. After getting settled in and finding out where everything was located, I was shown my barracks (or hooch as they would call them there), mess hall, outhouses, and showers. I reported to my company commander to find out what my duties/job would be. He said, "For now just report to your platoon leader, Sergeant Dallas, and he will line you up on our daily work schedule." Sergeant Dallas advised me that my primary job would be to operate a radio rig calling in air support for all our ground troops that were out in the field. However, he said when I'm not on radio duty, I would have other duties. So I asked him what they were. That's where I made my first mistake! He said, "Whatever I need done! It could be working in the mess hall, sandbag detail, guard duty, or working in the motor pool."

I could tell immediately that we were going to have a memorable relationship!

Sergeant Dallas sighting in M72 Rocket Launcher

595 Signal Co. Head Quarters in Phuc Vinh

During the hot summer months, the roads were extremely dry. With temperatures that would reach between 98 to 105 degrees every day, the dirt roads became like powder. Every step would send up little clouds of dust that covered your boots. Walking on them, you can actually see your own foot prints. Every night you would have to wash the fine powder out of every crevice of your body. Twice I had to go the field hospital on base to get my ears flushed from the red dust that would block my ear canals. The pain was so excruciating at times; it felt like my head was about to explode.

One day I was assigned to sandbag detail. That's where you go out to a sandpit sight outside our compound to have the local Vietnamese mothers (Mamasans) and the young girls (Babysans) fill your sandbags. We used these sandbags for protection around our tents and all our equipment in case "Charlie" (the Viet Cong) shells us with rockets in a mortar attack. It was early morning, right after breakfast, when Sergeant Dallas came into our tent and said he was looking for four volunteers for sandbag detail. Earlier, I overheard some of the guys saying that sandbag duty was one of the easiest jobs you could get. So, naturally, I didn't want to get stuck with a really crappy job, so I shot my hand up and said, "I'm in, Sergeant!"

So I myself and three other guys from our platoon—Dan, Red, and Sam—made up the team. Sergeant Dallas told Red to go over to the motor pool and get a "duce and a half" (two and a half ton) cargo truck. He soon returned and picked us up, and we headed out of the compound to the sandpits. Red was driving, Sam was riding shotgun, Dan and myself were riding in the back.

Mamasan's at sandpit to fill sand bags

Big Red at sandpit with Mamasan's

After filling and loading what seemed like a thousand sandbags, we headed back to the compound with our truck overflowing. Our load consisted of approximately three hundred sandbags weighing an average of 35 pounds, bringing the total weight to over ten thousand pounds. We were totally exhausted from loading all those bags, and none of us was looking forward to unloading them when we got back. On the drive back, I myself and Dan, were in the back of the truck sitting on top of all the bags when off in the distance another truck coming from the opposite direction came barreling toward us at a high rate of speed. I said to Dan, "Wow! That guy is really driving fast!"

As his truck passed ours, the air was filled with a huge amount of dust and sand from the bone-dry roads, sending rust-colored clouds of powder in all directions. The dust was so thick that we couldn't even see each other. Dan said, "Why do you think he is in such a hurry?"

"Maybe he's trying to get away from something or someone?" I said.

Little did we know at the time, but the thick rust-colored fog made it impossible for our driver Red to see where he was going. He couldn't even see the road in front of him, causing him to lose his bearings. We must have been traveling around thirty-five miles per hour when all of a sudden, we ran off the road and into a drainage ditch, stopping us on a dime. Our front axle hit a cement drain pipe. The truck fell to its side, throwing Dan and I into the ditch and all the sandbags came right on top of us both. As we were lying there at the bottom of the ditch, covered with sandbags, all I could think of was, *What just happened, and how do I get out of this mess? Was I still alive? Was anything broken? Can I still breathe?* Before I even had a chance to ponder those questions, the sandbags began to push its weight down on me. Slowly crushing me. Everything was eerily quiet except for Dan. I could hear him screaming at the top of his lungs. His voice trembling and filled with terror. He kept yelling, "I can't breathe!" and "I'm going to die!" He kept repeating it over and over again. I could feel the weight of all those sandbags getting heavier and heavier on me as well. They were literally crushing us both to death. We could hardly breathe, but I knew I had to reach out and try to comfort Dan and try to keep him calm. All that I could think to tell him was "we will be okay. Someone is coming, and you're not going to die." I used what little breath I had to repeat over and over, "Dan! You're not going to die! Someone will get us out of here."

But he kept screaming, "I can't breathe. Please, someone help me!"

By now I wasn't even sure he could hear me. The air was steadily being forced from my lungs, and now they began to burn from lack of oxygen. However, by trying to keep Dan calm and get him to save his air till help came, I found it helped keep me calm and in control of my own fear.

But now, the weight of the sandbags were getting so heavy I was forced to take shallow breaths. I was beginning to think Dan might be right, "No one is coming." Everyone must have been hurt and the truck that passed us just kept going. After all, how could they know we crashed with all that dust? And here we are in the middle of nowhere, with the threat of the enemy all around. It could be hours before they sent anyone to look for us, and by then, we all could be dead. In that moment, I knew that only God could help us now. We were all alone! Slowly being crushed. I never thought I would die this way. I began to pray, "God, please help us! Let someone find us and free us!" Over and over again I repeated that prayer for what seemed like hours. We must have been buried for fifteen to twenty minutes, but when you can't breathe, it seems like eternity. Dan stopped yelling. He was completely quiet.

My first thought was "he must be gone. I'm next." I began feeling numb and knew that I was about to pass out.

But *wait!* Was it getting lighter? I thought I could hear voices! I held my breath to listen more closely. I could hear very faint voices calling, "Are you there? Are you okay?"

"Yes!" I called back the best I could.

Please hear me, I thought! *God! Let them hear me!* I pushed with all the strength I could muster against the weight pressing down on me and tried to take in as much air as possible. With all the air reserves left in my lungs, I called as loud as possible, "YES, I'M HERE AND DAN IS HERE TOO!"

The voices got louder. "Someone's in there! Keep working. Get those sandbags off them!"

I could begin feeling the pressure lighten on my body. Breathing was getting easier. Then I saw daylight shining down on me. It never felt so good to be alive! I felt like God was placing his hand on my shoulder and saying, "I'm here. You're going to be okay, and I'm not done with you yet." I can honestly say, "If I've ever felt the love of God, it was in that moment. I *knew* he heard me, and I *knew* he cared."

Later, I found out that our driver, Red, was thrown from the truck on impact when he struck the drain pipe, and he injured his collarbone. The other soldier, Sam, riding shotgun (passenger seat) was thrown through the windshield. He landed on a large rock and broke his arm. We were all in a very bad place at that time. No one had the ability to help anyone. But by the grace of God, the truck driver who passed us said he felt that something was wrong. He didn't know why, but he just knew that he needed to stop. As soldiers, we were trained to never stop on a road outside of our compound. Chances of getting ambushed by the Viet Cong were extremely high. This gut feeling of his, however, was so overwhelming, he stopped the truck anyway. The soldiers on the truck began yelling at him, "What are you doing? Are you crazy! We're going to get in trouble!"

But he stood his ground. He knew he *had* to stop. He yelled back, "Wait a minute! Wait till the dust settles so I can see. Something is wrong! I just know it! I think I heard something."

When the dust finally settled, they all could see our truck lying on its side at the top of the ditch. They jumped off their truck and ran back to the ditch where our truck was precariously balancing over us. To their amazement, they couldn't believe that it hadn't rolled over on us. They radioed into camp for help and began calling out to see if anyone was still alive in the pile of sandbags. Then they heard Red and Sam call out to let them know that there were two guys riding on top of the sandbags, and they must be buried beneath them all. They began to lift off the sandbags as fast as they could. With all their help and by the grace of God, we were saved. Dan passed out but recovered fully. Me, on the other hand, I got out without a scratch, but I'm not sure why. God only knows for sure.

Dan on left and Sam on right on Motor Pool duty

Life Lesson Learned

By giving others who are in need of hope, you are giving them the assurance that they are not alone. God is always with us every minute of every day, and he will always give us strength to overcome anything we encounter. And by helping others, you will find a sense of calmness and peace just in knowing that you are doing the right thing.

> "But they that call upon and hope in the Lord shall renew their strength. They shall mount up with wings like eagles; they shall run and not be weary; they shall walk and not faint" (Isaiah 40:31).

My Second Encounter

While I was stationed in Phuc Vinh, Vietnam, I was assigned to 595th Signal Company attached to the first Army Division (Big Red One). For the first four months as a communication expert, I was working within the walls of our compound. I would watch a platoon of ten guys go out once a week right around 12:00 p.m. to patrol the perimeter in order to protect us all from the enemy. Eventually, I found myself feeling guilty about all the soldiers going out every week doing a twenty-five-mile sweep to keep "Charlie or VC" at a distance while I sat safe within the compound. I asked Sergeant Dallas and a couple of my buddies about these perimeter patrols. They told me anyone could volunteer, and Sgt. Dallas said he would go with us if we were serious about going. So after being there for two months, I decided to volunteer as a radio operator and join them on a sweep mission. We had to leave at noon and go out about two miles to patrol a ten-mile area every day. Boy, was that a mistake! I soon realized that being a radio operator was not a good job because you became a human target for "Charlie." Every time we came under fire, all I could hear was what I thought were bees whizzing around me. I quickly realized they were actually bullets. The Viet Cong would look for the whip antenna from the radio knowing that just beneath was the radio man. If they could take out the radio man, they would knock out our communications. Once they did, they knew we couldn't get any additional support. From that time on, I decided to volunteer as a platoon wing man in our V formation. My job was to cover their back. This meant that I would be carrying an M60 machine gun and have a soldier assigned to me to carry all my extra ammo! Every day, we would do a ten-mile sweep mission before dusk. Then we would find a safe place to bed down for the night. We would always choose a well-hidden area and take turns watching guard in two-hour shifts. Two hours doesn't seem very long, but when nine other guys are depending on you to keep them safe, it seems grueling. It takes every bit of focus and hyperattention staring out in the jungle, looking for any movement at all. I couldn't wait to be able to just shut off my brain and get some sleep. The most challenging obstacle in this situation is controlling your imagination. In high stress, hypersensory scenarios such as listening intently to the sounds of the jungle at night, the mind tends to play tricks on you. The wind blowing through the trees becomes the enemy sneaking up on you. The feeling of being extremely vulnerable like sitting ducks is constant. In Vietnam, the enemy owned the night, and they used it to their advantage. It was one of their greatest weapons. In the mornings, I can remember waking up, and all my clothes were soaked from the dew that settled on us because the humidity was so very high. We knew that every morning, our march to our next site would be brutal. With the temperatures reaching one hundred degrees, you could see the steam rising from our clothes. At times, it felt like I was like walking in a sauna bath. Add the dust and dirt to the formula and you have one miserable experience.

Art on patrol

Art with Frank the platoon radio operator

With my weapon and all my gear, I was carrying over fifty additional pounds. I was constantly hot, sweaty, and faint. After a week in the field, the anticipation of returning back to the compound made the march back seem endless. The thought of going back to camp kept me going. Finally, after five to six hours, I marched back into the safety of the compound. Finally! A good night's sleep, some dry clothes, and good food. I don't think I have ever taken those for granted since.

After a couple of months of these sweep missions, I and Sergeant Dallas received orders from General William C.

Westmoreland. He heard from "Intelligence" that the North Vietnamese Army was moving a large amount of their troops and equipment down south, and the Marines needed some air support on the DMZ "Demilitarized zone" due to a very likely attack on the south from the north. Vietnam's DMZ is the area around the former border between North and South Vietnam. Historically it was a narrow band of terrain extending from Laos to the coast, five kilometers on either side of the Bến Hải River. This area would find heavy fighting during the war. That meant they were going to need a larger communication network set up-and *soon!* So on November 15, 1967, I myself, Sergeant Dallas, and ten other communication specialists that were handpicked from all over Vietnam were sent to a city near the DMZ called Quang Tri. Our mission was to set up a communications network to call in air and ground support in the shortest time possible for all the Marines and Army soldiers who were on the ground on or near the DMZ.

Shortly after our entire communication network was up and running, I ran into a former buddy from my old unit in Phuc Vinh. He was sent up to help support our unit with extra man power. He informed me that the night I left to come up here to the DMZ, our compound was attacked by the Viet Cong and were completely caught off guard. It was around 2:00 a.m. when it seemed like the sky was falling down on them. Round after round of mortar rained down into the compound. Startled and half-dazed, everyone started running for some kind of cover, grabbing their riffles and any gear they could find. He said my bunk inside our barracks took a direct hit, and two of my best buddies were injured. He told me it was my best friend from Chicago named "Big Red" and Sam from Kansas City. These were the same two guys from the sandbag detail. They were injured but would be okay. What also broke my heart was when he told me about our camp dog (Sandy). She was the cutest little puppy that I found one day while on guard duty. I brought her back to my barracks, and from that day forward, she slept next to me when I was there. He went on to tell me that Sandy was killed that night in the very spot where I would have been sleeping. In that moment, again, I had been spared, and Sandy lost her life instead of me. The thought sent chills down my back.

Art's dog "Sandy"

Art's tent in Phuc Vinh with bomb shelter in front

The compound took over two hundred direct hits that night with a lot of men killed and injured. He said it took them over six hours to get everything under control.

"It was so bad," he said, "that we would have been over-run if it hadn't been for the help from our outside perimeter patrol and air support."

All I could think of was *If I had been there, I would have been right where Sandy was, and I would have been killed!* Was it just luck, or was it through the grace of God that he put me here? I was starting to believe that there was no such thing as luck. Once again, I knew God wasn't through with me yet.

Life Lesson Learned

When you think things are getting worse sometimes, it could be a blessing in disguise. When you find yourself in a bad place or a very uncomfortable position, just remember that when one door closes, another will be opened. God doesn't want us to be comfortable; he wants us to grow. He knows that we don't grow when we are comfortable, and because he loves us, he will always do what's best for us. So stay open-minded. Keep all your options open because when the time comes, and you are needed, he can use your talents to help others. We all become a stronger person for all that we experience, even though it doesn't make sense at the time. Everything happens for a reason. We just don't know what the reasons are. "Only God knows what our future holds and what his plan is for us." Trust in *him!*

Since I know it is all for Christ good, I am quite happy about "the thorn" and about insults and hardships, persecutions and difficulties. "For when I am weak, then I am strong-the less I have, the more I depend on him" (2 Corinthians 12:10).

My Third Encounter

It was on January 29, 1968, and while I was stationed in Quang Tri Province, which is only fifteen miles south of the DMZ (Demilitarized Zone), my name came up on the duty roster to pull guard duty in the north tower from 8:00 p.m. to 8:00 a.m. the next morning. This tower was twenty-eight feet high, and I could see for two to three miles easily on a clear night. I had night vision goggles called "starlight vision" binoculars. These allowed me to see equally as well at night as it does in the day, if not better. That's if the sky was clear and the stars were out.

My other equipment included an M60 machine gun and two boxes of ammo with three hundred rounds in each box. I also took my M16 riffle with two clips. I felt ready for anything and secure about doing my guard duty. Things had been quiet for the last ten days, and I had no need to believe that tonight would be any different, especially because our company commander heard that both the South and the North Vietnam had announced on National Public Radio that there would be a two-day cease-fire during the Tet Lunar New Year celebrations. This New Year holiday would be celebrated by both the North and South Vietnamese, and they would lay down their weapons during that time calling for a cease-fire. Plus, I knew I didn't have to worry about my sergeant checking up on me. He never checked the towers.

That evening began like any other. I got cleaned up and went to the mess hall to get some dinner and headed for my post around 7:45 p.m. to relieve the soldier on duty. We exchanged a few words, and I climbed to the top of the ladder with all my gear. I did a quick perimeter check, and then settled in for a long boring night. I was thinking, *I'm all by myself, and now I can kick back and relax. I can check on my buddy's pulling guard duty in other areas by using my walkie-talkie as long as the sergeant wasn't listening in.* We all knew how to keep track of the Sergeant. As soon as he was done with his rounds, the last guy would let everyone know that we were clear to talk. Anytime we had a chance, we would talk to each other about what was waiting for us back home. It would make us feel less lonely when we shared stories about our fast cars, the band we might have played in, or the girlfriends or wives we had waiting for us back home. We all looked forward to the end of our tour and go back to our families and the lives we left behind. However, my first and most important job was to keep a close eye out for any movement outside our perimeter. Now, all is quiet, and as the dark of night closed in, we had to focus on our job at hand. Another quick check confirmed that all things were calm as usual.

I'm not sure what time it was, but it had to be early in the morning, just before dawn when it seemed darkest. I was getting very tired and could hardly keep my eyes open when I noticed something very strange! The entire ground seemed to be moving. I rubbed my eyes and looked again. *How can the ground be moving*, I thought? We were taught that when you get tired and have a hard time focusing you should look to the side of the object you are looking at, which will help you to verify any movement. Yup! Everything on the ground seemed to be vibrating. I still had a hard time believing it. I got on my radio to see if anyone else could see the ground moving like I did. Just as I was about to transmit, all *HELL* broke loose! Radios were going off. Everyone was yelling! "The VC is tunneling up in the middle of our compound!" The next thing I knew, the enemy was jumping up from the ground right in front of me. They camouflaged themselves with bushes and tree limbs attached to their bodies and started charging our compound. They were screaming, blowing horns, and beating on what sounded like pots and pans. We were caught completely by surprise. The attack was perfectly planned right down to the phony cease-fire announcement. And now, they were right on top of us shooting and screaming. I did everything I could to hold them back, but they kept coming in waves. Shooting desperately from left to right and back again until all my ammo was out, but they kept coming. I was experiencing what I found out later was a human wave attack. I would shoot the ones in the front, and they would fall, but the soldiers behind them would step over their bodies and keep coming. Wave after wave after wave. *How many could there be?* I thought. *I must have killed hundreds, but they still kept coming! This can't be real!* Then I picked up my riffle and emptied that as well. Now with no more ammo, I was a sitting duck up in my tower with nothing to protect myself. The adrenaline was pumping, and I was just reacting. *What do I do now?* I dare not come down from the tower because I would have been an easy target and shot and killed for sure. All I could do was huddle down in a corner in the fetal position and pray. I felt totally and completely helpless. My body began to tremble with fear so intense, tears poured down my cheeks.

"Dear, God! Please save me!" I must have called out to him a hundred times. The gun fire and yelling continued. I could hear bullets strike the tower. I kept my eyes fixed on the doorway that opened to where I was. Surely, they would send someone up here to secure the tower! *What would I do? What could I do?* But miraculously, not one of them came up the ladder. All I could think of at that moment was there is no possible way I could get out of this. I'm going to die! So I did the only thing I knew to do was to have faith and to put my trust in God. I kept my ear glued to the radio to hear what was going on beneath me in the compound and prayed, and boy, did I pray!

"Dear, God, please let me put all my trust in you, and help me get through this. Please let no bullets or mortar shells hit me or my tower!" At that very moment in my prayers, I told God, "If it is your will that I live through all this, then I promise to always go to church every Sunday to show my thanks." I know I've said that before, but this time it came from my very soul. Because in the following moments, I came to realize that it is not just going to church that we find Jesus. He doesn't want me to go to church to just sacrifice my time, money, or to pray, listen to the gospel or the sermon. He doesn't want me to enjoy the music or any entertainment the church offered me. He wants us all to only go to church/mass on Sunday to receive and consume him in the flesh through the sacrament of Holy Eucharist. It is then and only then, he truly enters into our lives. For this is what he told us at the last supper: "Take this bread and eat it for this is my body" (Matthew 26:26).

For this is the food for eternal life! When I am present in you, I will give you joy, hope, and sense of peace and calmness. In that moment, when receiving Communion, I could feel the Holy Spirit in me strengthen me and giving me the courage to do his work.

Just then, I heard the other guards on the perimeter talking on their radios.

"They're hitting us on the south side hard. We can barely hold them back."

I could hear someone say, "They are coming up through the ground, and we are trying to push them back into the tunnels. We got help coming to support the north side, hold on!"

I could hear bullets whizzing overhead, shooting, coming from every direction and mortar shells exploding. Once again, I made a solemn promise to God right then and there. "I'll be the best Catholic I can be! I trust in you, oh Lord, to get me through all of this and to get me home."

The fighting seemed to last for hours. I remember lying there on the tower floor thinking to myself, *This isn't fair. I haven't had a chance to live my life. I haven't had a chance to start a family or career!*

All my dreams were fading fast without any hope in sight. After hours of fighting, things seemed to be getting quieter. Then I heard another guard over the radio say, "We're pushing them back on the north side." I thought to myself, *THAT'S MY SIDE! There is hope at last.* The sun began to come up. I'm not sure how long it was before I heard the "all clear" over the radio, but it didn't come soon enough. The announcement I heard was "the compound is secure, regroup and reload!" I got down from my tower as fast as I could and ran over to the ammo supply room, and got in line to get more ammunition. The Sergeant in charge barked out orders to hurry, get your ammo, and get back to your post! I was back in my tower all loaded and ready in a matter of only ten minutes. All stayed calm on our side for the last few hours of my shift. The enormity of what just happened began to sink in as I gazed out over the perimeter. I knew what I had done and looked for the bodies of those I shot. To everyone's surprise, not one body could be found. It seems that they picked up every body and carried it away with them so we couldn't count the number of kills. Later, when I was relieved of my duty on the tower, I talked to the guy that took over my post.

He said it was unbelievable, we were all sleeping in the compound when we were awakened by everyone on the perimeter, yelling, "We are under attack, and their coming up through the ground!"

The first thing we had to do is to get those tunnels plugged up so we pushed them back with our tunnel rats. These are our soldiers that would go into the tunnels and detonate explosives to seal them off. We learned later that the Communists launched a human wave attack all through South Vietnam. By the next morning, the offensive was countrywide and well-coordinated, eventually more than eighty thousand Communist troops struck more than one hundred cities in South Vietnam. This was the largest military operation ever conducted by either side up to this point. The initial attacks stunned the US and the South Vietnamese armies and caused them to temporarily lose control of several cities. Since then, I have asked myself how I could have possibly survived one of the deadliest attacks of the war. Many of my friends lost their lives or were severely injured. At times, I would feel guilty for having survived without a scratch, but part of me knew that God had a plan for me. Maybe if I knew what it was, I wouldn't have felt so bad. *Maybe, one day*, I thought, *I will understand. But for now, I will remain thankful and remember to keep those heartfelt promises I made to him, alone and frightened in that tower.*

Guard tower in Quang Tri Army base camp

Life Lesson Learned

No matter how bad things seem to be or how unfair life can seem, always have faith that God is right there with you. Have confidence knowing that he is guiding and helping you grow in strength and character in order to use you for his future plans. Never take anything for granted; your life can change in a second. Live each day like it's your last, because it just might be. And do the best you can for yourself and others. Make every day count by always trying to improve yourself and being the best version of you. No matter how close the enemy is or how close you are to death, know that God is always closer. He hears you, loves you, and he cares about your well-being. I still have that holy card, but now when I look at it, I think, *My mother was right when she said, "Keep this card close for the risen Lord will raise you above all harm."* I'm sure she didn't have any idea how many times he would raise me above all harm.

> "I will hide in God, who is my rock and my refuge. He is my shield And my salvation, My refuge and high tower. Thank you, O my Savior, for saving me from all my enemies. I will call upon the Lord, Who is worthy to be praised; He will save me from all my enemies" (2 Samuel 22:3–4).

CHAPTER 3

Skin Disease for Life

After surviving the TET offensive, I thought I could handle anything. That was the farthest thing from the truth. One month later (February 28, 1968), I broke out with a strange kind of rash. It started slowly at first. I began feeling an itching on my legs. The next day I noticed it began spreading to my butt, and then to my private parts. Try scratching there in public! But this was no laughing matter. I began getting concerned. Next, it spread to my chest and arms. Now I was *more* than concerned. I was scared. It began spreading more rapidly. It soon covered my whole body from my neck down. Even between my toes, fingers, and under my arms. In only a few days, red pus filled, and oozing, it covered every inch of my body except my face. The disease looked almost like chicken pox. Open, running sores that were very itchy. All my buddies were afraid to get near me knowing that this could be very contagious. They seemed very concerned not just about themselves but for me as well. I was told by several of the guys and Sergeant Dallas that if they can't find out what it is and don't have a cure, I won't be allowed to go home and have to remain here in Vietnam. Now I'm getting really scared! Sergeant Dallas reported my condition to our company commander, and after he saw me, he immediately cut orders for me to be medevaced down to the army hospital in Da Nang. That was the closest medical facility that had a doctor of dermatology. The company commander had a jeep drive me immediately to the airstrip where I was escorted on a C130 medevac plane to Da Nang. When arriving, I noticed quite a few wounded soldiers that were being loaded on the plane. Once we were all boarded, I looked around and noticed how they converted our C130 troop carriers into medevac planes by making bunks 3 and 4 high on each side to better transport the wounded. They would hold over seventy wounded soldiers on each plane. These were all young soldiers who were shot or wounded out in the field of combat. I got on the plane last, because all the wounded get loaded first. As I sat there watching all these young men pass in front of me, I was suddenly feeling very humbled and grateful, yet all I could think was that this is the last place I wanted to be.

I was already scared enough wondering if I would ever go home. And witnessing firsthand the ravages of this war only contributed to that fear. For hours I sat and listened to the groaning and screams of pain from these wounded and dying heroes. I could smell the dried blood, burned flesh, and saw missing arms and legs and bodies wrapped in blood-soaked bandages. My eyes began to well up with tears for these guys knowing that their lives would be changed forever. I lowered my head and swallowed hard to fight back the emotions. For some reason I felt like maybe God put me here to learn something from these guys by making me strong and giving me hope. On the other hand, I asked myself, *How could a loving God allow this? Where is he now, and why is he having all of us go through this?* My heart was breaking as I sat listening to these poor men, kids like myself, just out of high school, yelling and screaming for their mom or wife and pleading with God to save them. For the first time since I got there, I found myself praying for someone else. I wasn't sure if it would do any good, but I knew that if God could help me, he could help them too. For the next hour I asked God to help them and help me realize that no matter how difficult the situation we find ourselves in, we can always find someone worse off. I began to put everything in proper perspective. I needed to get over myself and thank God for only having a skin condition. I was beginning to realize *why* God placed me on that plane and why I developed a skin disease. One of the toughest lessons I ever learned took place on that plane. He didn't create me to be self-serving, but to serve others. He wanted me to feel deeply the pain of their suffering so that I would be able to recognize it in others and reach out and comfort them in their greatest time of need. So I continued to pray for all the troops on that plane and to thank God for looking over me and keeping me safe so that I would be able to step into his purpose for my life, whatever that might be. A little while later, we landed, and I knew when I stepped off that plane, I was a different man.

I reported to the hospital front desk and handed the nurse my papers to see a dermatologist. She told me to have a seat. It would be probably around two to three hours before I could see someone because they were so busy and taking patients by priority. I wasn't in any hurry anyway. I had four more months to go before I could go home. *Home!* What a beautiful word! *Home.* It became even sweeter with the thought that I may never see it again!

Sitting there waiting, my mind was all over the map. What if they couldn't find a cure? What if I couldn't go home? What if I never saw my wife or family again? How could I possibly live *here*? They must have some idea of what it is! I can't believe I'm the first one to get this. Maybe by the grace of God the doctors will find something to get rid of this itching and these sores that now covered my whole body. The nurse finally called my name and told me to go to room 8 down the hall on the right. When I opened the door, the doctor was finishing up his paperwork from his previous patient. He glanced over to me and told me to take off all my clothes and have a seat on the table. And so I sat there feeling like a naked leper. A few minutes later, he turned to me, introduced himself as the only dermatologist in the hospital, and apologized for taking so long. I said that was perfectly fine and very understandable with everything that's going on. He took his time, looked me over very thoroughly, and said he thinks he knows what it is that's causing my skin lesions.

The doctor said he hasn't seen anything like this here in Vietnam. But he thinks he did back in the States, and wanted to check his records to make sure it was the same symptoms he saw before. Now I'm really nervous! He's not sure, but he *thinks* he saw this once at home, *somewhere*? So now what happens if he can't find anything!

I couldn't help but thinking what the guys in my unit said, "If they don't know what it is you won't be able to go home!" It seemed like a month passed before he came back. I wasn't sure if I was shaking because I was naked and cold or scared of what he would say when he returned.

About half an hour later, he returned, and said, "I got it!" Number one, it's not contagious. Number two, it could take a while to clear up. It looks like you have a skin disease called "lichen planus." He told me all he could do for it is to give me some medication to relieve the itching and my immune system will have to do the rest. Eventually, it should go away all by itself. Of course, I asked, "If the itching goes away and I stop scratching, how long will it take for it to go away? I have four months left before I rotate to go home."

He said, "I'm not sure. It could take months or it could take years."

That's *not* what I wanted to hear! I was not happy. All I could think of, *If this doesn't go away before I get home, my wife will never want to get near me. This is so disgusting to look at! I looked like a freak with leprosy.* The doctor gave me the medicine, wished me luck, and said to come back if it doesn't get better. Now there's a vote of confidence!

I left the hospital thinking I need to get rid of this somehow. I was feeling desperate, so on the plane all the way back to my base, I prayed, "God, I'm in need of your helped again. I know I have been asking you for a lot, and there are guys over here that need your help more than me. But you know I just got married, and I don't want my wife to be freaked out and reject me. So, if it's your will, let it be done. But for the sake of my family, please heal me. Amen."

When I got back to my company, I reported to my commander and told him that my skin disease is not contagious and gave him my medical records. As he was reading about what the doctor wrote, I told him, "This medication will stop the itching, and over time it will go away. I'm just not sure how long it would take. The doctor said he wasn't sure either, but wanted to see me back in four weeks."

When I got back to my barracks, I told Sergeant Dallas and all the guys that my condition was called "lichen planus" and how the medication would make the itching go away, but the sores and lesions could take years to heal.

About four to five weeks later, the itching stopped, but the sores where still there and didn't seem to be getting better at all. I began thinking, I might be expecting too much and overreacting. Maybe I should be more patient, and eventually this will go away. But I needed to see some improvement; after all, I only had a couple of months before I could go home!

The next day, after having dinner in the mess hall, I went back to my tent. As soon as I walked in, the guys started teasing me and saying, "At ease disease! The fungus is among us!"

They weren't trying to be mean. They were just trying to be funny to make me feel better.

Then Sergeant Dallas called me over to his tent and said, "Have a seat. I want to have a serious conversation with you. I know how bad this is starting to bother you, and I just may have a way to help you get rid of this more quickly, or at least make it look a lot better.

I sat there on the edge of my seat all wide-eyed. "What is it? I'm ready to try just about anything."

He said, "With my experience in the service, I've seen a lot of things and a lot of guys with all kinds of medical conditions, and I remember this one guy who had a skin problem very similar to yours. We didn't know what it was either. He said he heard about a treatment that sounded really bazar, but he was willing to try it, and it *worked!* He did something you won't believe, and probably won't try."

I was so excited I could hardly wait to hear. So I said, "All right already, what is it he did?"

"Okay!" he said, "but you're going to think I'm crazy. Every night when he would take a shower, he would pee in a wash cloth and rub the urine all over his sores, and eventually they got better. Evidently the uric acid has some kind of effect on the disease and helps the skin heal faster."

"WHAT! Are you crazy! Do you really think I'm going to do that?" I looked him straight in the eye and said, "There is no way I'm going into the shower and do that just so you and the rest of the guys can have a good laugh."

At that point he said to me, "I wouldn't tell anyone, so who's to know? You'll be in the shower by yourself with no one around. We would have no idea if you did it or not, so what do you have to lose? Just try it!"

That night, I was playing poker with a couple of the guys. I kept thinking about what the Sergeant told me and was going back and forth in my mind whether or not I was going to try it. The night wore on, and it was getting close for lights out. I started to think of taking a shower before bed, and maybe I would try the pee trick.

No! What am I thinking? This isn't going to work. But, who was I kidding? I needed to try anything to get this to clear up. So about an hour later, I was off to the shower. While I was in there, I decided to try it. After all, no one will know what I'm doing, so why not? It just might work. I was getting pretty desperate, with only months before I go home.

Lo and behold, about a week later, after showering and washing my whole body with my urine every night, I started to notice a difference. All the redness started to go away, and by the time I was getting ready to rotate back to the States, I saw a great improvement. All the redness was gone, and the sores started to heal and dry up, but I was left with a million scars all over my body. I'm still not sure why it started to heal so fast, the medicine, the urine, or a combination of the two. I was just grateful for the improvement. However, it still took about three years for most of the scars to go away. Even though I wasn't hurt physically by the war, the memories I brought home with me will leave scars that last forever.

Life Lesson Learned

Always lean toward God. He knows what we need and when we need it! "It's not about what people think. It's about what God thinks that really matters."

Knowing now all that I saw and experienced is what gave me PTSD. But that's okay because I truly believe it made me who I am today. A soldier in Christ who is more sensitive and understanding of others and what they could be going through themselves. My transition to civilian life was extremely difficult for me because I thought I had lost everything. I allowed myself to become bitter and angry with God for so long that I shut him out.

I turned to alcohol and marijuana just to make myself feel better. But in reality, all it did was prolong the pain and loss. What I needed was the healing power of Christ to help me deal with all the trauma I had experienced. Once I turned my life over to him, I began a long journey that allowed me to come to terms with all the pain I was blaming on him. Now, I'm able to help others with their problems. I still fight with mine, but on a much smaller level. I've learned over the years how to deal with my PTSD. I did that by keeping myself busy with major projects like building a career in sales, business, religion, health, and building strong relationships with family and friends. I encourage everyone who even thinks that they may have PTSD to go and seek help at once! You can't do it alone!

Some people have said to me, in a kidding way, that I have an obsession toward things. But I call it being focused on what God wants me to do and to do it to the best of my ability!

> "So do not fear, for I am with you;
> do not be dismayed, for I am your God.
> I will strengthen you and help you; I
> will uphold you with my righteous right
> hand" (Isaiah 41:10).

CHAPTER 4

Unknown Virus

After I finished my combat duty in Vietnam on June 15, 1968. I was shipped stateside to be discharged at Travis AFB in Oakland, California. Then I traveled to San Francisco to meet my wife Nancy. It felt so good to see her again. She was the main reason why I looked forward to coming home. After we settled into our hotel room, I asked her to get me caught up on everyone back home. She said, "I'm sorry to tell you this, but while you were away, your mom and dad got divorced." They told me not to say anything to you while you were away. They wanted you to stay focused on your job so you could get home safely.

Wow! That took me totally by surprise. I knew they were having problems, but I thought they were working them out. They bought a new home and were trying to make a fresh start together. They sent pictures of them together in the new house, and they looked so happy. They sure fooled me! This started me thinking, *Is there anything else that has changed while I was gone?* A few days later, we left San Francisco and flew home to Detroit, Michigan. We lived with my mom and brother Rick for the next six months. With all my back pay and Nancy's savings, we bought a small house. It wasn't much, but it was a cute 1250 sq. ft. ranch in Madison Heights.

Shortly afterward, I went back to work for my dad and uncle Ed and picked up right where I left off. My first day back to work was brutal. Their company grew so fast while I was gone; they moved into a new building four times the size of the first one that I started. With so much more work, they had to hire a lot more people and even started a second shift. I thought I was set for life working in our family business. But that's not how they saw it. My dad told me that I had to work on a cutting machine and cut wire for the harness department at $3.50 an hour. I said, "What! Are you kidding me!"

He said, "No, that's all we have available. If you're not happy with that, you need to talk to your uncle. He owns most of the company."

I told him, "After everything I have done for the both of you to get this business started, this is how you are going to treat me? You had no one else you could trust."

My dad said, "Sorry! You need to talk to your uncle."

I said, "I *will*, and I stormed into his office. When I opened the door that said "President," I saw my Uncle sitting behind his desk talking to one of his supervisors and going over a blueprint.

I said to him, "I'm sorry for barging in on you like this, but I need to talk to you right now."

He said, "Sure," and asked Chuck, his supervisor, to step out for a minute. Then he said, "Okay, how can I help you?"

I began to tell him, "After everything I did to help you get this business started, then getting drafted and being sent to Vietnam, and now you want to put me on a cutting machine for $3.50 an hour? This is how you want to treat me? I don't think so!" Standing my ground, I said, "I deserve to be treated better than that."

After hearing me out, he said, "Okay! What do you think you deserve?"

I said, "At least $600 a month, and the position of supervisor of the wire cutting department."

He said, "Fine. We will get you started Monday morning."

I turned on my heel and walked out. As I heard the door slam behind me, I remember feeling like I only had a partial victory. Deep down inside, I was crushed because I was betrayed by my own family. Even after all these years, I still feel uneasy whenever I think about how I was treated by people I was supposed to trust.

That first year being home was a very difficult adjustment for me and Nancy. It seemed that everything had changed. Nothing was the same as it was before I left. In two short years, Nancy had gotten a job and learned to be independent. My mom and dad were no longer together. My childhood home was sold, and I returned to a different home in a new community. I felt like I was alone in a new and confusing world that I didn't like much at all. Looking back now, I realize how badly I had PTSD. Slowly, it crept into every area of my life. It began to take its toll on our marriage. I found myself becoming more withdrawn and secretive. I began keeping things to myself, and I wasn't honest about what I was doing or where I was going. Communication between us eventually became nonexistent. We tried to keep our marriage together by going to a counselor at the Catholic Social Services, but that didn't do much for either of us. We both thought that if we had a child, it would somehow change the other person and mend our fractured relationship. So on September 1, 1969, we had a baby girl—Kimberly Sue David. She was absolutely beautiful. I never knew I could love someone that deeply. She was the highlight of my life. I thought now we are a true family. I figured that Nancy would see how much I loved our little girl and come to love me the same way. I just knew we would be okay and live happily ever after. And, for a while, things between us seemed to be getting so much better.

What we didn't realize, however, was that the love we were feeling wasn't for each other but for our daughter. But as time went on, it became evident that nothing between us had changed; we just filled the emptiness by pouring our love into Kimmy.

Not only was I upset by the things going on at home, I was becoming very dissatisfied with my job. Each day became a real challenge. My dad and uncle weren't working together very well, making it extremely difficult for me. I could see both sides, and I just didn't want to have to choose. It just became too hard for me to work for family. So I shared my feelings with my brother Rick about what was going on, and he told me about this new health club that just opened up called "Silhouette American Health Spa." He knew I loved to workout and said that they were looking for instructors and hiring right now. It was located on Woodward Avenue in Royal Oak, just a few miles from my home. He said, "This is a great fit for you."

So I decided right then and there to quit D.C. Electronics and applied for a personal trainer's position. After my interview, I was hired on the spot and started the next week. Little did I know that it was more of a sales job than a personal trainer's job, but I knew I could handle that too. I was so excited! I went home and told Nancy that I was certain that if I enjoyed my job, things at home would *have* to get better. On my first day, I met Steve Anderson, the club's manager and one of the most dynamic men I've ever met. I admired everything about him. From the very beginning, he told me that he believed in me and knew with the proper training, I could be a superstar. So he became my first mentor and sales trainer. Together, we climbed the ladder quickly. He became the president and co-owner of the health club chain. It took me a little longer to achieve success. You see, this was my first real experience as a sales person. We were not only instructors (personal trainers), but we were salesmen focusing mostly on selling lifetime contracts. I thought it was a great job! I loved working with all the customers and got a great deal of satisfaction helping them to reach their personal goals. I would think to myself that I could be here for a long time and maybe even make it a career. I would go to work from 10:00 a.m. to 10:00 p.m. six days/week, and after the gym closed, we would count up all our sales contracts we sold. If the whole gym sold an average of ten memberships a day for a whole week, Steve would take us out for a steak dinner and drinks to celebrate. After seven months into my training, Steve told me that they were opening up a new club at 8 Mile Road and Kelly in East Detroit, and he wanted me to manage it for them. I was so excited and felt like I was really moving up the ladder of success. Little did I know that life was about to throw me a curve ball!

I had been working at the health spa (gym) for about a year when out of nowhere, I became sick. It was on a Monday around 2:00 p.m. when I began feeling light headed and dizzy. By 8:00 p.m. it got even worse, and I started feeling like I was going to pass out. By the time the gym closed, Steve said to me, "Boy! You sure look bad."

I told him all my muscles hurt, and I felt tired and even a little faint.

He said, "Maybe you should take a whirl pool bath, go home and go right to bed."

That sounded great, so I took his advice thinking I would be fine the next day. But I didn't quite make it until morning.

Then the fire of hell hit!

By 3:00 a.m. the next morning, I was in so much pain I couldn't even move. I tried, but nothing would move. The only thing on my body that seemed to still work was my lips. The pain got so bad that I screamed out to my wife to help me! I told her I couldn't move. She was so scared and asked me what was wrong. I told her I felt paralyzed! Every inch of my body was in so much pain I couldn't move. I said for her to call my brother and my dad to help me get to the hospital. It was impossible for her to help me because my body was like dead weight. She would have never been able to help me to the car. About half an hour later, my brother and dad both arrived at my house. They saw me in bed, flat on my back, face up looking very scared and in pain. My brother asked what happened, and my dad wanted to know how I felt and where I was hurting. I told them both that I hurt all over; every joint and every muscle in my body was killing me! It felt like a fire was raging through my body. I can't move anything! Not even a finger. They said they would try to pick me up and carry me to my dad's car and put me in the back seat and lay me down. As soon as they started to move me, I cried out in pain. I thought I would pass out. The pain from just moving me was beyond anything I ever experienced. I felt it throughout my whole body like someone was burning me with a hot poker in every joint. The ride to the hospital was incredibly painful. I could remember feeling every bump along the way. It felt like it took hours, but eventually we arrived at the emergency entrance. They got me a wheelchair and very slowly transferred me. Several screams of pain and lots of tears later, I forced myself to sit up so they could wheel me in. Once I was admitted and given a room, the nurses started an IV and drew some blood. The doctors ran numerous tests to see if they could find what was causing all the inflammation and pain in my joints and muscles. The doctors came back into my room after the results came back from the lab. They said that my white blood cell count was through the roof, which meant that my body was fighting some kind of infection, and it was attacking my body. They were not sure, however, what it was and needed to run more tests.

The protocol for disease control at William Beaumont Hospital in Royal Oak was extremely high, and they immediately put me in an isolation room in quarantine. All they knew for sure was that they didn't know anything for sure. It was something they had never seen before, but they thought it could be very contagious and even deadly. They were not about to take any chances. It was days before I could even have my family members come to visit. Every test they ran came back negative, so they began to ease restrictions a bit. On the days I would get visitors, either family or friends, they all had to wear protective clothing from head to toe. Even all the staff had to take extreme precautions. Finally, after a couple of days, the doctors called my family together to inform us that they couldn't find what it was that was attacking my body. They said it was definitely something very infectious because my white blood cell count was still very high. But they said they're not giving up and would keep looking by running more tests. In the meantime, they explained all they could do for me was try to make me comfortable with IVs filled with some heavy-duty antibiotics and painkillers. After about a week, Nancy came to my room and told me that a friend of mine—Paula O'Halloran—had everyone at the Shrine of the Little Flower church praying for me. She said the priest was also going to say a mass for me because they thought I was dying. And at that time, it felt like I was! Again, I found myself totally helpless. It seemed that no one would be able to get me out of this one.

Every day, I just laid there wondering if I would survive this. Nothing seemed to be helping. I wondered if I would ever stop hurting. I asked myself, *Is this the way I'm going to feel for the rest of my life even if I do survive? Did God rescue me over and over just to have me spend my days bedridden?* The thought was unbearable. *I was so confused and depressed.* I wasn't sure I could go on. The only thing that kept me fighting was the thought of my little girl and how she would need me growing up. This was a battle I knew I would have to fight on my knees, so I began to pray and ask God to heal me. I remember saying, "God, please help me through this! I have so much to do. I have a child, a wife, and a family who need me! God, I love you so much. Please give me a chance to make you proud of me by being the best version of myself." Day after day I would go to him and beg for complete healing. I knew he heard me. He's rescued me many times before, and I believed he could do it again.

It must have been two and a half weeks of suffering when I woke up one morning feeling nothing! No muscle pain. No joint pain. No fever. No back pain. *Nothing!* I remember like it was yesterday. As I started to wake up that morning, I realized that I didn't feel any pain. I could move my fingers, my arms, and my legs. I felt like I never had a problem at all, nothing. Absolutely nothing hurt. The nurse walked in, and she looked at me and was shocked to see me sitting up smiling, and I told her I felt great! Like my old self. I was full of energy, and I had no pain anywhere. She ran and got the doctor. The doctor couldn't believe that he was looking at the same guy that he saw the day before. He told me that they were going to check my blood count and run some other tests to determine what just happened. He ran a blood panel and several other tests to compare the results with the previous day. After the results came back, he said, "Everything came back normal. We have no idea what it was that attacked your body. But whatever it was it is 100 percent gone, and we have no reason to keep you in the hospital, so I am going to discharge you." He smiled and said, "You can go home."

So I asked the doctor, "If you don't know what it was, can you tell me what was it that made me better?"

He said he had no idea! He said for all he knows, it could have been all the prayers and the grace of God. They didn't know what it was or how to treat it. Shortly afterward, I was discharged and walked out as if nothing ever happened, and to this day, I have never had anything like that again. Thank you, God!

After all that I went through, I had to pause and reflect about my life and where I was going. I had a lot of quiet time laying there in the hospital. So I started to think of other things to keep my mind off all my pain and my depression. The one question that I kept asking myself was, *Am I on my own path, or was I on God's? What was he trying to tell me? Was he testing me? Was he strengthening me?*

I decided that what I was doing wasn't pleasing to God, and he put up a roadblock in my life that caused me to just stop. Working at the gym was fun and rewarding, but was it good for me and my whole family?

I was working twelve hours a day, six days a week, staying late to work out or going out with all the guys afterward. This was not a life for a married man with a child. I believe that God had given me another chance to get on the right path. I decided to quit my job at the gym and look for a new job or a new career. It was time for a new start and a new life. One more pleasing to God!

Life Lesson Learned

Another wake-up call from God!

The way you go through life and how you handle the obstacles determines your destiny. Where you place yourself mentally is where you will live physically.

So the way I see it, we should always think in a positive way, and walk with a smile on your face because God always has you in the palm of his hand. Not only does knowing this make you feel good, but maybe you can make someone else feel good too by just smiling. When you think you are all alone, in pain, and nowhere to turn, God shows up! Sometimes it's in a hospital bed; and at other times, it's a soft voice just before you fall asleep. Either way, he is always trying to get your attention, because he wants you to turn to him and ask him for help. All you need to do is trust in him, and he will do what is best. Sometimes he has to redirect your path to get you back on track. Believe me when I tell you, he never gives up. He wants to give us all joy, peace, love, and hope no matter what the situation. No matter how hopeless things seem, believe that he *can* and *will* work all things together for your good!

> "'For I know the plans I have for you,' says the Lord, 'They are plans for good and not for evil, to give you a future and a hope'" (Jeremiah 29:11).

CHAPTER 5

Spin Out on E-Way

After years of trying to make my marriage work, Nancy said she wanted a divorce. She wanted her independence and said she had no need for me and didn't love me anymore. We separated for a year, and then we were divorced. I was devastated and depressed. I kept hoping and praying that we might get back together one day. It took me years to build my self-confidence back up. Then I met Cathy. The most wonderful girl in the world that truly loved me and believed in me. She came from a strong religious family. She was a good Catholic girl that believed in God, marriage, and family the way I did. I knew she was the one I could build my new life with, so after two and a half years, we decided to get married. However, we faced an uphill battle with her parents and the church the entire time we were dating. I had three strikes against me. First, I was seven years older than Cathy. Second, I was divorced; and third, I had a child. Needless to say, her parents weren't happy. They told her to get rid of me. Thank God, over the years they came to know and love me. As it turned out, they were the most loving, caring, and supportive parents one could have hoped for. As for the Catholic Church, that's another story for another time. We both wanted to be married in the church so badly, I did everything I was asked in order to get an annulment. But the church wouldn't give me one, so we got married by the local justice of the peace. Things seemed to be on the right track for the first time in a very long time. I had a new wife, new job, and a new life! For the first time since I came home from Vietnam, I began to feel real joy. I believe God sent me Cathy to bless me for all the suffering I had been through. And then he blessed me again with a son, Jeffrey, and beautiful daughter, Kelly. I believe in my very soul that in those moments that I surrendered my life to him, everything changed. He began to show me that his plan was so much better than anything I could have possibly imagined.

Just when I thought my close encounters with God were over, he showed up again to show me that I was slipping off the path he set before me and how much he cares. It was in the spring of 1985 when my brother Rick moved to Columbus, Ohio. He accepted a position at Wendy's world headquarters in the training department. He was training new franchise owners how to run a Wendy's restaurant. It only seemed natural then that he would feel the need to start his own business. I remember the day he called me all excited about this great opportunity. It seemed he had the dream but didn't have the initial investment. He was looking for partners that could invest some money in the toy store business. Cathy and I had only been married about seven years at that time. We had two precious children—Jeff, five and Kelly almost four. I really wasn't in a position where I should be taking any financial chances. But Rick can be very persuasive when he wants to be. He told me and our father that if we invested $10,000 each, we would be a 1/3 partner in a toy store, which he would be fully responsible for. His wife would manage and oversee the day-to-day operations, while he took care of all the accounting and provide a monthly profit and loss statement. He said he knew of the perfect spot in an up and coming shopping mall with no competition at all. If things worked out as projected, we should show a profit in our second year. So dad and I agreed we would invest in his idea. We called our store the "Toy Box" located in a very popular and new shopping mall area in Columbus, Ohio. In order to meet our budget and have the store open in early summer that year, we decided to build our own display and shelving racks. My wife, Cathy, and my friend Roger volunteered to help me build theses shelves/racks out of the wire spools that my dad had at his factory that they were throwing out. They were perfect for shelving with 30" diameter wooden ends and a 12" center core. We worked on them in the basement of our house every day after work and on weekends till we got them done. I think they looked like they were very professionally done. We made them three to four spools high, painting all the surfaces with a high gloss white enamel paint, and carpeted the center core with bright colors. Then we bolted them all together to make them either three or four levels high. We decided that when we were finished, we would rent a trailer from U-Haul and drive them down to Columbus ourselves to save money. We were so excited! It was hard work, but we knew it would be worth it, because we were going to be owners of a very prosperous toy store. After three months of hard work, we finally finished on June 3, just in time for our June 15 grand opening. The following weekend, I rented a trailer. It was about fourteen feet long, and all we had to pull it with was our new Chevrolet Chevette. If you remember that car at all, you know it was a very small four-passenger compact car. So when I went to pick up the trailer and have a trailer hitch attached, the owner of the rental service said to me that my car was just at the limit to be able to pull such a large trailer. I'm not sure he was being totally honest with me. What he should have said was "ARE YOU OUT OF YOUR MIND!" There is no way that little car should have ever been pulling a trailer. But I guess he wanted to make the sale, so he soothed his conscience by warning me to make sure I didn't overload the trailer and keep the speed down to forty-five miles per hour max. That Friday morning, we took the trailer home; and I loaded it to the max, barely getting everything inside, doing just what I was told not to do. But I had no choice, we had to leave now, and I had to get everything there by that weekend. It was a little after twelve noon, and we were on the road with just Cathy, my four-year old daughter Kelly, and myself. Our son Jeffrey, was staying at Grandma Salhaney's house for that weekend.

As we headed off, I was thinking, *This is going to be one of the most fun-filled road trips we will ever take.* We had a hotel lined up right in Columbus, only about two miles from the new toy store. I kept thinking how much fun it was going to be to set up all those shelves and put up all the displays and stocking them. With the grand opening day on Sunday, this was getting so exciting. We left early and headed for I-75. Traffic was light, the sun was shining, and we settled in to our four-hour trip. A couple of hours later, I was talking to my wife, Cathy, about all the things we needed to do. We both got all caught up in the conversation, not realizing I had started to speed up. Before I knew it, the trailer started to sway from side to side. I immediately looked down at the speedometer and noticed that I was going almost seventy miles an hour. I knew that was way too fast, and I needed to slow down now. Cathy said, "What's going on?"

By now, I was in panic mode. I couldn't even talk! I was just trying to stay focused on the road and what I was doing. I tried to slow down to stop the trailer from swaying, but that made the trailer sway even more. It was too late. I looked in my rear view mirror and noticed that all the traffic around and behind us slowed way down, as if they knew what was going to happen next. All of a sudden, the car started to spin out of control. The only thing I could do at that time was to hold on to the steering wheel, lock my elbow into the door to prevent it from slipping out of my hands, and pray. I could feel the trailer pulling us back and forth, tossing us around like a rag doll. The landscape was spinning around us like we were on an out of control merry-go-round. My heart was in my throat. I could feel my hands begin to cramp from gripping the steering wheel so tightly. Then all I remember seeing were signs spinning past, then the concrete median, then the cars that had stopped behind us! As uncertain as my future was in that moment, one thing I knew for sure was, "we are going to crash!" The car was still moving as we headed for the shoulder. I was certain that if we hit the shoulder or any signs, we could flip. *How could I put my family in this kind of danger?* I thought. Around we went. I could hear the tires screaming and smell the rubber burning. We did a 180-degree spin in the middle of the I-75 expressway. This was the heaviest traveled road between Michigan and Ohio at noon, and the chances of surviving a crash were slim to none. And yet, as our car came to a complete stop, we ended up on the right-hand shoulder of the road facing the oncoming traffic with the trailer directly behind us. Miraculously, we were completely unharmed. We never hit another car, sign-post, concrete barrier, or overpass. What are the chances of that happening?

We sat there stunned. Each of us wondering what just had happened? None of us spoke a word for what I thought was a long time. I believe we were just grateful for being alive. Then Cathy and I heard this little voice from the back seat say, "Daddy, are we okay?"

We looked at each other, sat there for a moment, took a deep breath, and I said to my little daughter, "Yes dear. We just got turned around. Now with God's help, we will be more careful and finish our trip." I looked over at Cathy and said, "That was one scary moment."

All I could think of was how God held us in the palm of his hand, held all the traffic back, and guided us to the side of the road. Needless to say, I watched my speed very carefully the rest of the way there, staying in one lane, never moving.

I guess it wasn't our time. God has more things for us to do. Still not sure what that might be.

Cathy and Kelly at the Toy Box

Life Lesson Learned

When traveling through life, we should always stay focused on all the signs that God sends us by paying close attention to the people around us. *We* should listen only to those who lift us up. God sends us messages and warnings through others. I now know that God tries to communicate with us in so many ways and keep us on the right path. The path that leads us to a life of joy and happiness, which can be experienced as long as we stay focused on him.

From time to time, I will look at that holy card my mother gave me—"The holy card of the risen Lord"—and know it is Jesus that I need to focus on. He promises to guide and protect us all. And once again, he has shown me, beyond any shadow of a doubt, that he keeps his Word!

> "The Lord will keep you from all harm—he will watch over your life; The Lord will watch over your coming and going both now and forevermore" (Psalm 121:7–8).

CHAPTER 6

Angels Looking Over Us

It was 1983, three weeks before Christmas, Cathy and I were doing some last-minute shopping with our children. Jeffrey was only four at the time, and our daughter Kelly was two.

It was one of those typical winter days in Michigan where it was cold, snowy, and windy. We didn't pay much attention to the weather. It was Saturday, and we had some last-minute Christmas shopping to do, so we packed up the kids and headed to the mall. We only had a few more people left to get gifts for, and we thought the mall would be the ideal place to go. Everything we needed would be in one place. It would be perfect for us, all indoors with a lot of different kinds of stores all under one roof. Once we arrived, we realized that it seemed everyone else in the area had the same idea. After three excruciating hours, we both thought it was time to make our final purchase and call it quits! Fighting the crowds and dealing with hungry and crabby kids was beginning to take its toll on us. Cathy said we had only one more gift to find, and then we could leave all this craziness. It seemed hundreds of people were packed in every store, and all the checkout lines were backed up thirty or so deep. My patience was being stretched to the limit, and dealing with irritable kids and pushy, rude people trying to get in their last-minute shopping was the real test. We finally "pinballed" our way to the toy store for the last gift. "Thank you, Lord."

By now, both the kids had reached their limit and were ready to go home. As we worked our way through the crowded toy store, we were focused on locating that last gift and getting out of there! We knew what we wanted; now it was just finding it. But after thirty to forty minutes of elbowing through every isle and not seeing it anywhere, we decided to leave and try another store on another day. When leaving the store, I began to count heads to make sure we were all together. I made it a habit as we walked out of the store to make sure no one was missing. Okay, I can see Cathy has Kelly as I head for the door, and I am holding Jeffrey by the hand. We were all together as I made my way to the door and through the maze of people. As we were getting closer to the doorway, the crowd was getting tighter around the cash register, and I wanted to get a better hold of Jeffrey, so I decided to switch his hand from my left to my right. I let go of him for just a second and turned my back on him. But as I turned around to reach for him with my right hand, he was gone! Just that fast, one and a half seconds and he was gone. I was in shock. He just disappeared. Cathy was right in front of me, so I immediately yelled at her to stop.

"I lost Jeffrey!" I said.

She could tell by the look on my face I was serious.

At that point, I started to panic. Frantically I ran back in the store. Being only 5'6" tall, I couldn't see over the crowd, so I started jumping up and down trying to look over everyone, calling out his name.

"Jeffery! Jeffery!" I called over and over.

I just knew I would hear his little voice call back to me. But nothing. I was running and bumping into everyone, looking down every aisle and no sign of my little boy.

I remembered that earlier, he saw a toy that he wanted, so I reasoned that he might go back to get it. I rushed back to that section. Nothing! Losing a child in a crowd has got to be the worst feeling ever. *How could I? How irresponsible,* I thought. If anything happens to him, *I'll* never be able to forgive myself. Once again, I darted throughout the whole store and still nothing. I started to panic. I have felt helpless before, but nothing like this. It was like having part of you torn away. From the deepest part of my soul, I began to pray, "God, please help me find my son. I need you now more than ever!"

I knew he wasn't in the store, so I decided to expand my search out into the mall area. As I passed the cash register where Cathy was standing with Kelly, I could see the fear and concern in her eyes. She asked me if I found him. I said *no* and told her I was going out into the mall to see if I could spot him out there.

She sensed the panic I was experiencing and told me to slow down! "What we need to do is get the store manager to call mall security."

So while I was running all over the place like a crazy man, she told the cashier what had happened, and she quickly placed a call to security. The cashier asked Cathy to describe what Jeffrey looked like and what he was wearing. She relayed the information to security. We stood together waiting for security to call back. Another five minutes went by, which felt like five hours, and there was still no sign of my little buddy. I was looking to the left and to the right, back and forth, searching for a glimpse of my son. *How scared he must be!* I thought. All I could see was a sea of people in both directions. We were on the second floor of the mall, so I went over to the railing and looked down at everyone, hoping I would spot him roaming around looking for us, but still nothing. I went back to the toy store and saw Cathy with a security guard talking about Jeffrey and what they were going to do next. Then ten excruciating minutes later, the guard got a call on his walkie-talkie. Then the guard said, "THEY FOUND HIM! He is downstairs at the lower level of the mall at the security station located in the middle of the mall by the stroller rental."

We were so relieved! I could hardly believe it; all I could think to do was to say, "THANK YOU, GOD! Once again you heard me and answered. THANK YOU! THANK YOU! THANK YOU!"

I was so relieved. I could feel a huge weight lifted off me.

As we were approaching the security station, all I could see was my little boy sitting on the desk. As we got closer, I saw his little face. I could tell he was crying. As soon as he saw us, he had this look of confusion and wonder of why we would leave him alone. I felt so bad for him and so embarrassed for losing him. We asked the lady at the desk how they found him, and she said they didn't. What happened was an older man saw Jeffrey wandering around the upper level of the mall, crying, and he asked him if he lost his mommy and daddy. Jeffrey said he doesn't know where we went! The old man told Jeffrey not to worry; he will have the security guard find us. He brought our son right downstairs and took him to the security station, asking them if anyone was looking for a little boy. He knew what the answer was going to be. The security guard said, "Yes, the parents are waiting upstairs to hear from us. I'll give them a call and tell them that you found him, and he's down here. Do you want to stick around to meet them?"

He said, "No, I just want to make sure he finds his way back. I've got more work to do."

That seemed to be a strange answer since he clearly didn't work here. What I assumed he meant was that he had more shopping to do. Then he walked away and disappeared into the crowd. I couldn't help but ask myself, *Was this just a kind old man? Or maybe, just maybe, God sent an angel to find my little boy and deliver him safely back to us.*

Life Lesson Learned

I truly believe we all have guardian angels looking over us. So now I never take anything or anyone for granted, especially the people in my life, for they could be with us one minute, then gone the next. Cherish every moment you spend with a friend or a loved one for our time with them is uncertain. Let us always be more than thankful for the people God puts in our lives. For the people that cross your path in life could be an angel sent by God!

> "Beware that you don't look down upon a single one of these children. For I tell you that in heaven their angels have constant access to my Father" (Matthew 18:10).

CHAPTER 7

Finding God by Accident

May is an exciting time of the year for our family because we are boaters. Every year at this time, I go to the marina where our twenty-nine-foot Regal boat is stored/docked and get it ready for the season. There's a lot of work that needs to be done when you own a boat. I have to take off the stretch wrap, clean the whole interior, check all water lines, clean and wax top and bottom decks. I sometimes asked myself if it was worth it. But it only takes a few minutes skimming across the lake with the sun on my face and the wind blowing through my hair to reassure me that life doesn't get much better than this.

The day before my annual clean and prep ritual, I needed to load up my SUV with all the cleaning supplies, ladder, and a change of clothes. That way, I can just leave right from work and go straight to the marina. It was May 2006, I finished loading all my supplies, and I double checked just to make sure I had everything I needed to work on the boat that day. The last thing I needed to load up was my six-foot ladder to reach the upper parts of the boat. Finding room to transport it to the marina was another challenge. I decided that the best way would be to place it long ways behind the passenger seat. It just fit, so I closed the hatch and headed off to my first sales call for the day.

As the president/sales manager of our family business called Macomb Wholesale Supply Corporation, which is a wholesale distributor of industrial supplies as well as a full line of packaging and janitorial supplies, I would be on the road for part of the day, either training sales people or selling. The rest of the day I would be running my company from my office. That particular day, my first customer was so far away, I had to leave by 7:00 a.m. to be there by 8:00 a.m. While on the way, my daughter called me on my cell phone and asked me if I would pick up her computer that my son Jeff had with him. He graduated in 2003 from Oakland University as a computer engineer. He was working full-time for Macomb Wholesale and loved to work on computers for friends and family in his spare time. After making my sales calls for the day, I went back to the office and picked up my daughter Kim's computer that Jeff finished working on. Now I have a car full of cleaning supplies, a six-foot ladder, a computer, and a gym bag and one more thing on my "to-do" list. Next, I was supposed to head to the marina for a couple of hours of physical labor. But as I was finishing up my day's work, I started contemplating what I really wanted to do afterward. Did I really want to go to the marina and work on my boat, or go to the gym and workout? I guess I could always go to the marina tomorrow.

I'm what I guess some people call "health nut" and a "gym rat." I have always taken a great deal of pride in taking care of myself. Some friends have told me I'm a bit excessive, but I have always enjoyed exercise. I'm constantly looking for ways to improve my health. I usually go to the gym three to four days a week. As an outside salesman, I made a lot of sales calls all over town, which required a great deal of driving.

I found this would often leave me mentally exhausted, and stopping by the gym for a quick workout would rejuvenate me. This particular day seemed to be quickly wearing me down. All I wanted to do was go home and relax. However, my conscience got the best of me so I decided to go workout at the gym before going home. I convinced myself that I would get in a quick workout and take a relaxing Jacuzzi. I know how important it is to stay healthy for myself, my family, and my business, so I went and got an hour workout with fifteen minutes in the steam room and fifteen minutes in the Jacuzzi.

It seemed to do the trick. I was feeling a bit peppier and a little more relaxed, really relaxed. After my workout, I took a hot shower with a cold rinse to try to wake me up. I went back to my locker and dried off, got dressed, and headed out. *Skip the boat for tonight,* I thought. I just wanted to head home for a hot meal and relax for the evening. It was a very long day, and it was already after 6:00 p.m. Everyone was on their way home, and the traffic was so thick I had to wait for quite a while to find a clearing before I could pull out on the road. Once on the main street, I had to stop for the traffic light. I must have been behind eight cars from the light in the far left lane next to the median. I remember sitting there in my car, feeling really relaxed, and in a daydreaming state.

All of a sudden, everything went black! It was like someone just flicked a switch off in my head, and all the lights went out. I didn't hear a thing, just complete darkness and complete silence. This was unlike any silence I ever experienced. It was like I was out of my body and being suspended in a very dark space with a blank mind with nothing to think about, like I no longer existed, but I knew I did.

The next thing I was aware of was opening my eyes and seeing the blue sky with white puffy clouds. I was thinking to myself, *This is not good! Wasn't I just sitting in my car, sitting at a light?* It was as if I still wasn't in my body. Just then I heard a voice say, "He's awake!"

Then a fireman's head was looking over me saying, "Do you know your name? What is your address?"

I barely got out my name and address, when I saw an EMS person. They said, "Arthur, you were in an accident, and we are going to strap your head down on our board just as a precaution while we transport you to the hospital."

I said "Okay," but was thinking, *I don't feel like I was in an accident! What the hell just happened! I don't know how or why this was all going on.* Total confusion.

When I arrived at the hospital, they took me out of the ambulance and wheeled me on a gurney into the emergency room where Cathy was waiting. As they were wheeling me down the hall toward the X-ray room, Cathy asked me how I was feeling. I told her, "I feel fine other than my neck is killing me from my head being strapped down to this darn board!"

I wanted to know if they could take off the head strap, so Cathy asked one of the nurses, and she said they could only remove it just before going into the X-ray room. Then I asked Cathy if she knew what just happened.

"I hardly know anything about the accident," I said. "All I can remember was sitting in my car, stopped at the light right in front of the gym on my way home, when all of a sudden everything went black."

She told me she was making dinner when the phone rang, and when she answered it, she said a man told her that he was a minister. The minister told her, "Your husband just got in a car accident, but he is okay. They are taking him over to St. Joseph Hospital on 19 Mile Road, and you should meet him there. Here's my number just in case you need anything."

But she said, "I can call him back and ask him if he knows anything more."

I said "Would you, please? That sounds like a great idea."

When she called his number, he answered immediately and said, "I was wondering if you would call me back."

Cathy said, "I'm sorry for bothering you!"

He said, "No bother, how can I help you?"

She asked him if he knew anymore details of the accident.

He said, "I saw the whole thing." He then proceeded to tell Cathy the whole story.

"We were all stopped at the light on Schoenherr Road going north just before Hall Road. We were backed up at the light, and I was in the car right next to him. There was a small car who ran right into the back of your husband's car. He got hit so hard that it sounded like a bomb went off, and your husband was knocked out on impact. When I looked over, all I could see was his body slumped over the steering wheel and people running all around the car. I got out of my car immediately to see if I could help. I heard a lady shout out to everyone standing around his car, 'I'm a nurse. Don't do anything until the police and ambulance get here.' She could see that your husband was knocked out and laying over the steering wheel. However, in the next few minutes, she saw your husband was going into shock, having convulsions and shaking vigorously. She then said, 'This is not good!' and told everyone at that very moment that we need to get him out now! One of the guys in the crowd broke the back window so he could open the car, because it was still in drive, and all the doors were locked. Once he got the doors unlocked, they could get him out. At that point, he stopped shaking."

The minister said it was incredible how they took me out of my car.

"The nurse told everyone who was helping him out of the car to be careful because he was still unconscious, and he could have some internal injuries. So when they took him out of the vehicle, they were so careful. It was like watching someone that was floating on a cloud. As they were setting him on the ground, I heard the nurse saying to someone that she was following the guy in the little red car that hit him. Then a couple of people spoke up and said they also saw him speeding and swerving from one lane to another. The nurse said she was following him for three miles like that, just waiting for something to happen. He was flying up to the light where the traffic was all backed up. I heard her say he wasn't going to stop in time because he was going so fast, and he never applied his breaks at all. The red car ran directly into the back of your husband's SUV. He must have been going fifty to fifty-five miles an hour. The only thing that stopped him from going any further into your husband's car was the rear axle. I looked over at your husband immediately and noticed that he was knocked out cold and slumped over the steering wheel. His airbag never went off because he got hit from the rear first. It wasn't ten minutes later, and the ambulance showed up with police and fire trucks."

The minister said that's all he could remember but wanted to know how I was doing because he said he was praying for me right after that happened. My wife told him that I was okay for now but will know more after the X-rays. He said it's great, and he knows everything will be fine for God is with your husband. "But I will still keep praying for him."

After talking to the minister, a policeman came up to us while I was lying there waiting to get X-rays. He asked me if I knew what happened so he could finish his report. I told him that the only thing I knew for sure was what the minister just told us. So we proceeded to tell him everything the minister told us. After that, the policeman told us everything else that he knew about the accident. He said the man that hit me was alone in the car, and he was a diabetic that went into diabetic shock. This caused him to become unconscious just before hitting my car.

I could hardly believe what just happened, but it was all beginning to make sense. The policeman said, "The way your car was hit and how it looks now, it is truly a miracle that you are alive. Because your car was completely destroyed. The only part of the car that anyone could have survived in was the driver's seat. The area of the driver's seat was like a small capsule, completely intact, almost like you were being protected."

Rear end of SUV with ladder

Art's SUV accident

I immediately asked, "How the man was doing that hit me? Was the man okay? How is he doing?"

The policeman said, "Right after he hit you, the man was so delirious he got out of his car and started walking away. Because his airbag went off on impact, he never got hurt. Someone from the crowd stopped him and had him sit down and wait for the ambulance. When the paramedics looked at him, they found that he was diabetic and was in a diabetic coma. He went to the hospital and had his sugar levels adjusted. After that, he was fine. Back to normal."

"Thank God no one else was hurt," I said to the policeman.

Now the nurse came out and said, "It's time for you to get your X-rays."

The doctor did a complete body scan to see if I had any internal damage done. Then they put me back in the hall to wait for my results. At that point, I didn't care about the wait because they removed my head strap, and now my neck was feeling a lot better. So now the wait to see how much internal damage was really done. Cathy and I were sitting on pins and needles, anticipating the worst, like we all tend to do. After a couple of hours, we finally got the results of my condition. A doctor came up to us and said, "I got all your test results back, and after looking over everything thoroughly, I'm glad to say we couldn't find anything wrong. Now there's no reason to keep you any longer. You are being discharged and free to go."

I said, "You mean to tell me there is nothing wrong at all?"

He said, "Nothing we can see at this time. But keep an eye on things, and let us know if you experience any changes."

On the way home, Cathy and I were talking about how bazaar it was to be perfectly fine after an accident like that. We decided that it would be a good idea for me to go and see my chiropractor (Dr. Riffle) just to see what he thinks. The next day, I called Dr. Riffle's office, and I told the receptionist what just happened to me, and she placed me on hold while she went to speak with the doctor. She came back on the phone and said the doctor wants you to come in immediately to get a complete body check. When I got to his office, they had me come right in. The doctor looked at me and said, "Tell me everything that happen to you."

I told him the whole story and showed him the pictures of the accident. He had me lay on the table and looked me over from head to toe. He said, "I can't see anything that's out of place so far, but I want to do a full body MyoVision scan showing inflammation of muscle, ligament, or tendon damage."

He hooked me up to a computer with a lot of electrical wires and ran several tests and had the results sent over to a printer. After about fifteen minutes, he came back into my room where Cathy and I were waiting. He said, "I'm not sure exactly how to tell you this. But what you told me about your accident and how bad it looked and from the pictures you showed me, it's hard to believe what your tests show. It appears that you are in better shape now than you were a year ago when I saw you last. All I can say is, just be thankful because you have to have someone looking out for you. You have been truly blessed!"

At that very moment, I came to realize this was a wake-up call. *You have been saved one more time for a very special reason.* I thought to myself, *It's time to give back!*

Two weeks later, I was reading our local newspaper and ran across an article about this husband-and-wife team that was feeding the homeless at a local church. I was so taken by what I read on how they were running a kitchen and feeding over a hundred homeless people at St. Margaret's Catholic Church. I knew I needed to help somehow. I felt so strongly about this. I just knew that God was sending me there. Maybe this was my way to give back for all he has given me! That was the reason he brought me back from the war and saved me so many other times after that! He wants me to help others who are lost or struggling in life and help them find their way back to him. God is our Creator, and he brought us all here for a reason. And it's up to us to trust in him and to love him with all our mind, heart, and soul. I now know now that working with him and doing his work on a daily basis is the only way to feel true joy and happiness.

Life Lesson Learned

God's in control of everything!

Always give back what is given to you, because everything comes only from him.

We all find ourselves from time to time in a place where we think that things are really bad. *We* are not even sure why God is allowing this to happen to us. All we know is that he is in control of everything. Maybe it's to make us stronger, maybe to bring us closer to him, or show us that he is with us all the time no matter what we are going through. Whatever the reason he has, it is not for us to know but for us to trust and believe in him. This was my wake-up call to do more and get closer to him.

When I start feeling like I'm alone, I say these words, which help me feel closer and more confident: "O Lord, my God, in you do I take refuge."

> "Don't copy the behavior and customs of this world, but be a new and different person with a fresh newness in all you do and think. Then you will learn from your own experience how his ways really satisfy you" (Romans 12:2).

CHAPTER 8

Homeless Shows God's Love

After years of hard work and determination, God blessed me with financial, physical, and spiritual success. Don't get me wrong, it wasn't easy. There were more downs than ups, but in the end, God allowed me to build a successful business. Along the way, I never forgot to stay grounded in my faith. I kept those promises I made so long ago and came to realize that our God is a God of promises. He keeps his word and blesses those that bless others. I am reminded of a time when he showed me exactly how he works. I retired from our family business (Macomb Wholesale Supply Corp.) in 2008 when the economy was really bad. This was perfect timing for me and the company because now I was sixty-three years old, and I would be eligible to collect Social Security. That would allow me to invest my payback into the company. In order to stay afloat, our employees had to give up some of their pay as well. This would ensure that the bills would continue to get paid and prevent us from having to let anyone go. So for the last three years, while I was still there, I began to train my son Jeff to take over the family business. Three short years later, I knew he was more than ready, and it was time for me to move on. I was excited to see my son follow in my footsteps yet kind of sad to see a part of my life come to a close.

Two years earlier, I read an article in our local newspaper about a husband-and-wife team (Norm and Carolyn Johnson) at St. Margaret Catholic Church that started a soup kitchen and shelter for the homeless. The article was so inspiring to me that I went over to the church in St. Clair Shores to meet them. I wanted to see if there was anything I could do to help them with the cost of their janitorial and kitchen supplies. I told them that I would be willing to give them all their supplies for only 10 percent above our cost just to cover the paperwork, delivery, and driver. They were so thrilled that they started ordering that same day. While I was there, I wanted to learn more about what they did, so I asked them if they could show me exactly what they were doing for the homeless. Carolyn said she would love to give me a little tour of the facilities. She then explained that not only did they give the homeless people a hot breakfast and lunch, but they did their laundry, gave free haircuts, hot showers, warm clothes, boots or shoes if needed, and resources for health care and other needs. They not only saw to their physical needs but emotional and spiritual needs as well. Carolyn would often ask some of the homeless ones to help volunteer with check-ins, dispense toiletries, monitor showers, and do laundry. By showing them that she trusted them with some responsibility, she was building their self-esteem. She would always ask everyone to stand and form a circle, and she would address them and refer to them as family. She did her best to let them all know that she was there for them, and they weren't going through this alone. She always had someone step forward and read a passage of Scripture from the Bible before being seated for lunch. She always asked for prayer requests from the group and would always close by asking everyone to join hands and recite the "Our Father." Once all the homeless people were fed, she made sure they all got a sack lunch to take with them. I was so humbled by the experience. I knew I just had to somehow be a part of this. Here was the real heart of Jesus being lived out by everyone that joined this dynamic couple. I knew in my heart that God was calling me to help any way I could. St. Margaret's Pantry and Kitchen was only open Mondays, Wednesdays, and Fridays from 7:00 a.m. to 12:00 noon. They served them breakfast and lunch, which provided me the opportunity to step up and serve them any way I could. I told her that when I retire that I would love to volunteer there and help in their kitchen or anywhere they needed me.

So the very first week after I retired in 2008, I went over to see Carolyn. I walked right up to her and said, "I'm all yours! I've retired from my company, and I'm ready to start work wherever you need me."

She said, "Great! How about working in the kitchen?"

I said, "Sure, that sounds good to me."

She introduced me to the kitchen manager Debbie, who seemed excited that I was there. The first thing she asked me was if I would like to cook because she was always missing a cook and had to do everything herself. She said it was getting to be too much for her. It was a lot trying to manage the kitchen, make out the weekly menu, prep the food, and cook for over a hundred homeless people three days a week.

When I heard that "over one hundred people," I said, "Oh boy, I think I bit off more than I can chew!"

But she assured me that it would be no problem.

"All you have to do is have breakfast ready by 8:00 a.m. and lunch ready by 11:00 a.m."

"WHAT! No problem? Are you kidding me?"

She said, "Nope! I'm confident you can do it."

So I asked God for some help. "Lord, you put me here for a really good reason, so please help me put this all together."

As time went on, I found things were getting easier because Debbie now had time to have our menus and recipes ready for the next day. She also had a lot of the food picked up from the local store and prepped for the next day's lunch. All I had to do was to follow her recipes and have everything ready to go for the next meal.

Most of their food was donated, but she always had to get some ingredients to complete her meals. I came to realize that she was a true blessing, a gift from God. After working there for ten years, I can look back and see how God has changed my heart in so many ways from everyone in the kitchen, all the volunteers, and the homeless people as well. Most of all, I experienced firsthand how God can work through us to accomplish anything when we just trust him and step out in faith. Carolyn shared with me that she had no idea how she would do any of this but stands amazed every week at how our loving God provides.

It was approximately three months after volunteering at St. Margaret's that I heard about an organization called MCREST that stood for Macomb Rotating Emergency Shelter Team. It was a county funded program that provided temporary overnight housing for the homeless. I wanted to do just a little more volunteer work to fill in on the days I wasn't working at St. Margaret's. I thought this might be a place where I could do some good by helping the homeless on a more personal level. I felt my heart pulling me in that direction. I just didn't know why. I remembered what Carolyn told me, "Just step up, and watch what God can do."

So I thought, *If this is a place where God wants me doing his work, then that's what I'm going to do.*

MCREST would find a church that could accommodate housing for around thirty homeless people to sleep, feed, shower, and provide transportation for one to two weeks at a time. Volunteers from all over would help with various jobs. Some would help with check-in, help make food, or serve food. Some would stay overnight while others would volunteer to provide transportation to jobs, doctor appointments, or just drop them off at the bus stop or the mall.

So as the story goes, the second time I volunteered, I was a driver at a church in Sterling Heights called Redemption Lutheran Church. We were housing twenty-five men at the time. It was one of the coldest February mornings I think I can ever remember. I got up to a snow-covered day with very slippery roads. I got a cup of coffee and headed to the church. As a driver, it was my job to get as many people in my car as I could for my first drop off, which would be the local bus stop. When I was getting my SUV loaded with my second load of men, I noticed this one man. His name was Edgar. Edgar was a robust African American man around thirty years old. He must have been 6'6" tall and weighed about 290 pounds. When I saw him and how big he was, I knew he would be more comfortable sitting in the front seat next to me. There was no way he would even fit in the back. I yelled out to Edgar to sit in the front with me. He gave me the thumbs up sign and climbed in. There were four more guys in the back, all going to the bus stop where they would get a ride to a job, library, or their doctor's office. Because this was their only way to travel, MCREST would also give them bus tickets to get around. Once we were loaded in the SUV, I started heading off to the bus stop. Not long after we were on our way, Edgar started a conversation with me. He said, "By the way, my name is Edgar, and I've been on the streets for over two years now. What's your name?"

"My name is Art, and I just started driving for MCREST." Then I asked Edgar, "What happened to make you homeless?"

He said, "It all began to happen when I started having medical problems. I was working for Smart Bus Lines as a driver and one day I hurt my back. The pain was so bad I couldn't even walk. Then I started having trouble with my knees and after going to the doctors for two months, he told me that I'm going to need an operation. After being off work for so long, I lost my job."

However, I know this wasn't the whole story because it didn't all add up, and I heard somewhere that Edgar has some anger issues, which lead to alcohol, and then deep depression. However, I just listened, and let him tell his story his way. All I wanted to do was get these guys to the bus stop so I could get back to make another run. It was silent for about five minutes, and then Edgar said, "Hey, Art! You know when you were a little kid and your parents would ask you to make out a Christmas list of the things you wanted?"

I said, "Sure! We used to call it our wish list."

Then Edgar said, "I remember doing the same thing. If I could make out a wish list right now, I would put a pair of gloves on it just like the ones you have on right now."

Knowing how cold it was outside, I asked him if he had any gloves at all, and he said no. Nothing more was said after that. We soon arrived at the bus stop, and I let everyone out. On the way back to the church, I kept thinking about what Edgar said about the gloves. I felt so bad. Here I am with all the comfort one could ask for, and he had so little. I remembered what the church pastor said in our orientation class when we first started, "Do not give any homeless people money or gifts, because the church will provide for all of their needs. Otherwise, they might use it for drugs or alcohol."

All that night I kept thinking, *I need to do something.* All of a sudden, it came to me. I have some of my father-in-law's (Larry) clothes from when he passed away earlier that year. I remembered that he had a brand-new pair of gloves, and they were way too large for me. I could give them to Edgar. They would be perfect for a big man like him. So I told Cathy the whole story about Edgar and asked her what she thought about my idea. She said she thought that would be great that it would be typical of something that her dad would want me to do.

The next day, I went to the pastor and told him what Edgar said to me, and I happen to have a pair of gloves his size. So I asked if I could give them to the church to give to him, but the pastor said, "You can give them to him yourself if you like."

I said, "Are you sure? I don't want to break any rules of yours."

He said, "No, you go right ahead. That will be fine."

So once again, after breakfast, all the homeless guys got in my car to go to the bus stop. This time Edgar hopped right in the front seat. Before we pulled out, I said to Edgar, "Remember that Christmas list or wish list with the gloves on it that you mentioned to me?"

He said, "Yes."

Then I said, "Well, your wish is about to come true. Here are a pair of leather gloves for you just like mine."

He looked at me all wide-eyed in disbelief. I handed him the gloves, shook his hand, and said "Merry Christmas."

He was so overwhelmed he started to cry and said, "No one has ever done anything like that in a very long time for me."

After dropping everyone off at the bus stop, I made one more run with another group of guys, then I went home to pack for vacation. Cathy and I were going to Florida for ten days to get away from all the cold and snow in Michigan. When we got back, I noticed that I had a message on our answering machine. It was the pastor from the church where I volunteered driving the homeless guys. He said, "Hey, Art, this is Pastor Tim. Give me a call as soon as you get back from vacation."

I gave him a call right away, and he picked up the phone. I recognized his voice and said, "Hi, Pastor Tim. This is Art returning your call. What's up?"

He said to me, "You are not going to believe what I'm about to tell you. Remember those gloves you gave to Edgar?"

I said, "Yes!"

"Well, Edgar was so grateful for what you did for him that he went around to every homeless guy and took up a collection for you. He then took all the money and went out and bought you a Christmas gift."

In all my years of helping the poor and homeless people, I have never experienced a bigger gesture of love and kindness. To give up all they had for me was their way of saying, or maybe it was God's way of saying, "Keep doing what you are doing." I stopped by the church to pick up the Christmas gift and to my amazement, it was a beautiful big gift basket full of cheese, crackers, jelly, chocolates, and wine. I couldn't believe my eyes. Talk about humbling! This would have humbled anyone. Still to this day, I cry knowing what those homeless people did for me and how it brought me closer to God. About nine months later, I was working at St. Margaret's cooking lunch when someone came in the kitchen looking for me. They said, "There is a homeless guy out in the dining area asking about Art, and he is insisting to see you. I had no idea who it could be, so I went out to the dining room to see who it was and what they wanted. To my pleasant surprise, it was Edgar. Wow! I was truly happy to see him again. I had been wanting to see him so that I could thank him for the Christmas present.

Art with Edgar at Saint Margrets

I went up to him, and he gave me a huge hug, and he said it was great to see me again. He asked what I was doing there at the soup kitchen, and I told him I was the cook. He just smiled at me and said, "I thought it would be something like that."

I said, "Edgar, tell me something would you?"

He said, "Sure! What do you want to know?"

"I want to know why you bought me such a beautiful Christmas gift. All I did was give you a pair of winter leather gloves."

He looked me square in the eyes and, with all sincerity, said, "What you did for me touched my heart so much I wanted to touch your heart too!"

"You *did,* my friend!" I told him. I will always remember you and what you did for me.

"So will I," he said.

We gave each other one last hug, and then I watched his big frame lumber out the door.

"Dear God," I began to pray. "Watch over Edgar. Keep him safe, and please let him know that someone cares." With tear-filled eyes, I returned to the kitchen and continued cooking. It's those precious moments that show up out of nowhere that help make sense in the midst of all this suffering. As I drove home that afternoon, I thought of one of my favorite poems.

> When someone's lost, aimless and adrift
> Take the time, give 'em a lift
> Yesterday is history,
> tomorrow is a mystery
> But today, you can be their gift.
> —Squire Rushnell

Life Lesson Learn

Sometimes, the smallest things can merit the biggest rewards! I've learned humility and how being a humble person makes you a better person. This allows you to see the needs of others more clearly.

We are all hurting in some way, so it is our responsibility as one human to another to show each other compassion, kindness, and love. I keep thinking that this is what God sent us here for! Jesus said to us all that we need to do only two things that are most important to him. First, to love him with our whole heart, mind, and soul! Second, to love each other as we would love ourselves!

> "Do not forget to show hospitality
> to strangers, for by doing so some people
> have shown hospitality to angels without
> knowing it" (Hebrews 13:2).

CHAPTER 9

Finding My Purpose

Deep down inside, we all want to find our true purpose. That is when you feel your true passion. Our desires become fulfilled, and we begin to feel joy and happiness radiate all around us. We begin to feel a sense of peace and calmness deep within. *Wow!* Doesn't that sound great? Well, you might think that's impossible and that no one can feel like that. You may even think that's a fairy tale. For many years, I used to feel the same way. I was wrong. I discovered that when *I put myself first and believed what others told me, I never really could find my true purpose.* I found myself searching for something better, only to discover that it was right in front of me the whole time. The answer for me was putting God first in my life's journey. Every journey starts with the first step. The first and most important step is to make a *mind* and *heart* connection. The Native Americans used to say, "The longest journey for one is to make a heart and mind connection."

We can only do this through prayer. But before we begin, we need to know the meaning of prayer, and then we need to know how to pray. After all these years, I finally realized that in doing God's work, I found this feeling of true joy and happiness that I thought was impossible. But now I know why God has blessed my life so abundantly. It is because I started living my life and doing all my work for him and him alone. I began to stay close to him not only in my words and actions but also through prayer, especially through prayer. It is where we build our relationship with him. Jesus told us how to pray and what to pray daily.

That prayer is called the "Lord's Prayer." "Our Father who art in heaven, Hallowed be thy name. Thy kingdom come, Thy Will be done on earth, as it is in heaven. Give us this day our daily bread. And forgive us our trespasses, as we forgive those who trespass against us. And lead us not into temptation, but deliver us from evil. Amen."

The "Lord's Prayer" is the most moving prayer you can say because it comes from Jesus (God) himself. It is the foundation and main aspect of our faith that is summarized in several short lines. Let's take a closer look:

"Our Father who art in heaven."

He is everyone's Father, making us all his children. We call God Father when we pray, this sets up the same level of intimacy that Jesus has with his Abba (Daddy).

"Hallowed be Thy name."

May your (God's) name be held holy. That we may honor him first and everything else be set apart. For he is everyone's one true Father.

"Thy kingdom come."

For it is your kingdom "eternal life" that we seek.

"Thy will be done."

For it is your will for all of us to be loving only to him first and all others next.

"On earth as it is in heaven."

While we are on earth, we must commit ourselves to Christ. And by doing his work, then we can become one spirit with him.

"Give us this day our daily bread."

We ask God to not only give us the food we need to nourish our bodies, but also to give us the *Bread of Life*. "The Holy Eucharist" to nourish our souls.

"And forgive us our trespasses, as we forgive those who trespass against us."

God teaches us that he forgives all who come to him, but for him to forgive us, we must also forgive all others who we need to forgive.

"And lead us not into temptation."

We are asking God, our Father to set up roadblocks to keep us far from the path of temptation and sin.

"But deliver us from evil."

We ask God to shield us from the devil and all his evil in the world. And he will always protect us through prayer.

"Amen."

So be it. It shall be done.

I hope and pray that you find *your* true purpose, and with the grace of God, you feel all the joy and happiness that comes only from him.

St Augustine said: "You made us for yourself O Lord, and our heart is restless until it rests in You."

Today at seventy-four years old, I continue to volunteer three days a week at "St. Paul of Tarsus" food pantry.

Now I know why Jesus saved me so many times from life-threatening situations. I truly feel this is my destiny, or should I say, my life's purpose. I feel Jesus wants me to do his work by bringing others close to him. I can only do that by using the gifts he has given me and sharing my faith with others. Often when I do, I can feel his presence. It's that satisfaction that comes knowing I am doing what I was created to do. I often feel him when I am praying with others or just listening to our client's stories of how life's circumstances brought them to our pantry. It is like no other feeling I have ever felt before. I can see the pain in their eyes and hear it in their voices of how very hurt, sorrowful, and even lost they are. We tell all our clients not to worry, because God sent them to us for a very good reason. It is because God loves them so much. He wants them to find peace and joy in their hearts and in their lives. Not just receiving his food from our pantry, but by feeling his love from our hearts and to receive all his resources that we have available for them.

Our pantry director Darlene and I came up with a meet-and-greet team about one year after we worked at the pantry. This program allows us to meet with our clients one-on-one and build a relationship with each one of them. We try to put them at ease by asking questions that help us determine what's going on in their lives in order for us to better serve them. During the process, we try to discover how they got to this place and give them the tools that help them improve their lives. We assure all our clients that we will help them fulfill their wants/needs by guiding and supporting them toward total independence.

I've had the privilege to train some very special people to work with me on our meet-and-greet team. I say that because it takes special people who are compassionate, committed to help others, and have a deep love of Christ. People who are very secure in their faith and confident in knowing that God called them to serve in our pantry to do his work.

Myself, as well as all our pantry volunteers, derive a great deal of satisfaction by giving back for all that God has given us. We all continue to have our share of problems that life continues to throw at us, but we have learned to turn them over to Jesus. He gives us strength and guidance to keep moving forward knowing that he is always in control. Only when we give our best, love others, and love him, will we gain a sense of joy, meaning, and a true feeling of purpose for our lives.

When talking to our clients, we hear all kinds of heartbreaking stories. Everything from drugs, alcohol, desertion, loss of work, injuries, sickness, old-age problems, or just making bad financial decisions. There are all kinds of reasons that people find themselves on hard times. I just recently spoke to one of my clients, Peter, who was a soldier that served for many years in the Army. He had a lot of bad experiences in and out of active duty. This left him feeling abandoned and completely lost. He was living at home with his mother without a job and feeling angry about everything that life threw at him. He had all the signs of PTSD. He tried to get help from the Veterans Administration (VA); however, he said they couldn't find his records. This made him feel completely frustrated and not sure what to do next. He said after coming to our pantry and talking to me about my military experience, it gave him hope and the strength to stay persistent with the VA. Then finally, he found someone who helped him locate all his records. After he started working with the VA and with some therapy, he found a sense of calmness and purpose to his life. Now, today, he thanks God for all he has, and now he knows that happiness and joy comes in forgiving. First, in forgiving himself, and then all others who hurt him. We are not called to judge, but show compassion and share God's love by giving them hope, hope for a better life and a promising future by working with them and helping them through their personal crisis. We try to provide the resources to help them come up with a plan that allows them to move closer to independence.

Not only does our pantry help others with *their* lives, but it helps each one of us discover a whole new life with Jesus. Sure, it makes us feel good about what we do, but giving to others gives us a deeper, more meaningful connection. A feeling of certainty, a radiant glow of love that permeates our mind, heart, and soul. It goes to the very core of who we were created to be. I finally know I'm doing something really good and pleasing to him. It isn't every day, but quite often, I experience how Christ would touch someone's heart by using me. Every time he does, my spirit is flooded with an incredible feeling of gratitude. I become so overwhelmed on those days, I go home and share those life-changing moments with my wife Cathy. I always feel so excited when I can help someone feel good about themselves and help them find joy again. This is what we were *all* created for: to *love* others as he loves us. And helping the poor and needy is a sure way to experience his love and his presence! I never thought I would ever feel the love of Christ like this, but once you commit to him with all you have, he pours his abundant grace into your life. I often feel the presence of Jesus in the gratitude of others. Knowing that it is his way to give us encouragement and show us how he longs for us to come to him. One of the most inspiring letters I ever read was written by Saint Mother Teresa. Her commitment to sharing the love of Christ through her tireless acts of charity inspired me to dig deeper, push harder, and give selflessly. I hope by sharing her words with you, you can feel moved to begin to follow the kind of life that promises us the kind of joy and peace that can only be found when we surrender everything to the purpose for which we were created.

Saint Mother Teresa best explains it in her letter to us all.

"I Thirst, I Quench"
25 March, 1993

My Dearest Children,

Jesus wants me to tell you again, especially in this Holy Week, how much love He has for each one of you—beyond all you can imagine. I worry some of you still have not really met Jesus—one to one—you and Jesus alone. We may spend time in church—but have you seen with the eyes of your soul how He looks at you with love? Do you really know the living Jesus—not from books but from being with Him in your heart? Have you heard the loving words He speaks to you?

Ask for the grace, He is longing to give it. Until you can hear Jesus in the silence of your own heart, you will not be able to hear Him saying "I thirst" in the hearts of the poor. Never give up this daily intimate contact with Jesus as the real living person—not just the idea. How can we last even one day without hearing Jesus say "I love you"—impossible.

Our soul needs that as much as the body needs to breathe the air. If not, prayer is dead and meditation is only thinking. Jesus wants you each to hear Him—speaking in the silence of your heart. Be careful of all that can block that personal contact with the living Jesus. The devil may try to use hurts of life, and sometimes our own mistakes—to make you feel it is impossible that Jesus really loves you, is really cleaving to you. This is a danger for all of us. And so sad, because it is completely opposite of what Jesus is really wanting, waiting to tell you. Not only that He loves you, but even more— He longs for you. He misses you when you don't come close.

He thirsts for you. He loves you always, even when you don't feel worthy. When not accepted by others, even by yourself sometimes—He is the one who always accepts you. My children, you don't have to be different for Jesus to love you.

> Only believe—You are precious to
> Him. Bring all you are suffering to His
> feet—only open your heart to be loved
> by Him as you are. He will do the rest…

After reading that letter, I felt the need to come close to Jesus. I believe we all have the same need, but we just don't know where to start. Let's follow the advice of Mother Teresa when she said, "Open your mind and heart, then take action."

He is waiting for us to come to him and talk to him in prayer. Show him that you are there waiting and wanting his abundant love. Ask him to shine his light on your path so you can see the way he wants you to travel. Everyone of us can feel his presence when we commit to pleasing him by doing his work, not ours.

Life Lesson Learned

We all want to do good or even give back to God for all he has done for us. But life can be very hard at times, and we begin to have doubts. This can lead to feelings of depression, self-pity, loneliness, and low self-esteem. However, when life becomes a struggle, we need to remember that as Christians we have the Holy Eucharist to give us strength. It is in the receiving of the Holy Eucharist that we can experience the Holy Spirit come to life within us. Then, and only then, we can start to heal ourselves and, in doing so, help others begin to heal. To help me draw closer to the Holy Spirit and strengthen my relationship with God, I say this short prayer.

> We are the light of the world,
> Love is our only purpose,
> That is why we are here.

You are the light of the world,
Love is your only purpose,
That is why you are here.
I am the light of the world,
Love is my only purpose,
That is why I am here.

"For we are God's handiwork, created in Christ Jesus to do good works, which God prepared in advance for us to do" (Ephesians 2:10).

Techniques for Dealing with PTSD

Anxiety can impact every area of our lives in so many ways. It affects our memory, work performance, and even our relationships with loved ones as well. We can go online to find some type of free therapy that can help us manage our stress and get us in a more relaxed state of mind. Some of the other things that help me are breathing therapy (like Qi Gong breathing), emotional freedom technique (EFT) tapping therapy, or (yoga) meditation therapy.

For me, therapy is an awaking experience. So allow yourself to be awakened.

No matter if you're going through some difficult times or feel like you may have PTSD, never give up on yourself. Get help. We all need God's strength and support to seek the help we need. There are now apps and websites to get your own help. They show techniques to manage symptoms, get support, and learn how to track your progress. Simply go to apps and type in PTSD Coach, and start your own personal account. If you are, or have been, in the service, you can go online and type in ptsd.va.gov. Either one will help.

The Presence of God

As a teenager growing up in the sixties, it was so much fun! Shortly after graduation, everything began to change quickly. In a few short years, I was drafted, got married, fought in a war, had a child, changed jobs, and came home to a very different world. I felt like I was losing everything. I began to feel a separation of heart and mind. But through prayer, I found strength and hope. It's like Matthew Kelly said in his book *I Heard God Laugh*: "Prayer helps us make the journey from the head to the heart, and it is prayer that allows us to balance the heart and mind so that we can live in wisdom." As I sit here trying to think of a way to summarize this book and bring everything to a close, I find myself overwhelmed with emotions. My life was like being on a roller coaster. It began slowly, like going up a steep hill—never stopping, but making steady progress to the top. Once on the top, it was like my life was on top of the world. But within the blink of an eye, everything changed. I found my heart in my throat, plunging rapidly downward, fearing for my life. But now when I look back, I can truly say that God has blessed me in so many ways. All the stories and facts you read here are true. These stories are about every experience that I went through that brought me to the place I'm in today. I now live a much different life because of the realization of God's incredible love for me. Now I *know* he was with me every step of the way, walking right beside me, watching over me. It just took me a while to realize that it was him who saved me so many times, not by chance or Lady Luck. I can see how he helped me make good decisions every time I came to a crossroad in my life. For a long time, I took God for granted. I just thought of myself as one of the luckiest guys in the world. But in 2006, with my last eye-opening experience, I finally said, "Okay, God. I'm listening! Tell me what it is that you want me to do."

Once I said that, he began to open a lot of doors. I didn't sit waiting for direction. I set out to seek his presence by doing as much volunteer work as I could. I found myself asking, "Why did I wait so long?" It seemed I was waiting until 2008 when I retired. I told myself I would have more time then. But the truth is, I should have started sooner. I guess I wasn't ready to see all the messages he had been sending me my whole life. But with the car crash and how my life was spared against all odds, I knew his hand was in all this. I had the feeling that *this* might just be the *last* chance he was giving me to wake up and listen. In that moment, I knew I needed to do something right now to show my gratitude. Like most of us, I was a little slow to see how God was trying to tell me to pay attention! I guess he needed to use an old man to run into the back of my car to get me to listen. It worked! I thank him every day for hanging in there with me and believing in me to do his work and follow his direction. So when I retired in 2008, I made a promise to God that I would improve my life for him in two healthy ways. First, I would improve my health physically and second, spiritually. God loves us so much he wants the very best for us. He wants us to be healthy and happy in order to better serve him. Once

I made that vow, I began reading and watching videos on how to become the best version of myself. I knew that if I got in shape physically, I could work longer and be able to help others spiritually. I decided to change my life through a series of daily routines that helped me become a better husband, father, brother, and friend. I found that when we stick to a routine, it becomes a habit, and habits are what change us and tend to make us who we are—good or bad. That's why I changed. And now, I continue to follow the routine I started twelve years ago.

Here is the routine I found helps me stay on track, stay healthy, and prepare me to serve God every day. The first thing in the morning at 5:30 a.m. I drink 3–12 oz. glasses of purified water with turmeric. This not only gets me hydrated but purifies my body at the cellular level. While drinking, I also read the Bible for half an hour to purify my mind and be reminded why I am here. Then I do half an hour of yoga with deep breathing, stretching, and meditating. I find this helps clear my mind while building strength and energy. At 6:30 a.m. I have another 12 oz. of water and take my supplements. Now, I'm ready to start my day. I go to the gym and workout at least three days a week for two hours. I will always fast from food for sixteen to twenty hours a day five days a week, This is extremely good for the immune system. It stops all my cravings and creates more energy than I've ever had. During my eating window, from bout 2:00 p.m. to 7:00 p.m. I only eat healthy organic vegetables. I start with a high protein veggie shake and later will snack on raw veggies or my favorite fermented foods. Next, I will plan my plant-based diet dinner comprised of fish or chicken. I try to limit these animal and fish proteins to twice a week. At the end of my day, I try to be in bed by 10:00 p.m. That way, I know I will get between seven and eight hours of sleep per night. I can honestly say that my overall health physically and spiritually is better now at seventy-four than it was when I was forty. I can only thank God for this new life. I'm not suggesting that this will work for everyone. But it has for me! We all have different needs, but we all need to do the best we can to take care of ourselves. If this means you need professional help, then *get it*! You are worth it. God expects nothing less, but for us to give our best and to be good example for others.

Is this system perfect for me? No! But I'm working on it every minute of every day. We are all a work in progress, myself included. One thing I do know for sure is whatever you do, do it for God! When you do, he will reward you in so many ways. It all starts with love: love of God, love of self, and love of others. Only when we focus on those three things in that order, can we truly begin to live a life of purpose.

St. Augustine of Hippo said: "You have made us for Yourself, O Lord, and our heart is restless until it rests in You."

CPSIA information can be obtained
at www.ICGtesting.com
Printed in the USA
LVHW090825241021
701365LV00004B/60

9 781638 447054